THE NOBLER RISK

The Nobler Risk

AND OTHER SERMONS OF

AMBROSE WHITE VERNON

Selected and Edited by

ROY B. CHAMBERLIN

1 9 55

Dartmouth Publications

HANOVER · NEW HAMPSHIRE

Contents

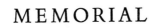

MEMORIAL

A MEMORIAL

"People about us speak and think all the time, but those who are most in earnest in their thinking *write* their thoughts in orderly and consecutive fashion." So spoke Dr. Ambrose White Vernon in one of his sermons, and that was apparently the principle determining his whole career. He not only insisted on writing his thoughts; but he kept what he had written. At his death in 1951, he left in manuscript form quantities of lectures and essays and letters, nearly six hundred sermons, and a long and complicated book, not yet published, to which he devoted his last years. Therefore, the main problem confronting his friends in preparing a suitable memorial was that of selection.

At first it was thought that such a volume should include at least examples of the various types of productive work that occupied Dr. Vernon's busy years, but such an idea soon seemed to be impractical. Where should one begin or end? Then it was suggested that the problem might be solved by confining the proposed book to the kind of creative work for which he had particularly prepared himself in studies at home and abroad, to which he gave his best years, and for which he was most highly honored, namely, his preaching. That was the decision finally made.

The sermons here presented come close to reflecting every facet of Dr. Vernon's genius and his vibrant personality. Almost every page bears testimony to the depth of his religious faith and his zeal in proclaiming the Christian Gospel, and to his unswerving but critical loyalty to the two historic institutions, Church and College, to which his life was dedicated—but only so long as the Church was a free one, and the College a liberal one. The reader is always aware not only of his reverence for sound scholarship and his fearless and disconcerting search after truth, but also of his love for the best in literature and the arts, and his familiarity with history on which he drew freely for illustrations; for example, his skillful sketches of great personalities, ancient and modern, anticipating his classroom work in the field of biography, are equally delightful and convincing to the reader. One is gripped by his unremitting demand that man must live by the ideals—Duty, Liberty, Truth, Love, Christ—which alone can make life noble. And all is done expertly, with the master touch of one who knew and loved words, whose literary gifts were of a high order.

It should be added, however, that the book is inevitably an inadequate memorial, simply because a sermon, or a collection of them, is only a part of a larger whole, and Dr. Vernon would be first to say so. It is unfair to take words out of context, and that is true of a sermon. The *whole* is the total experience of public worship of a living congregation, and it includes the esthetic, the ethical, the intellectual. Without the context of worship, with its carefully chosen organ and choral music, hymns, prayers and lessons, a sermon may be little more than a literary gem or an eloquent address.

Each of Dr. Vernon's sermons is preserved in a manila envelope, half-size, often dog-eared and darkened by age, on which is inscribed the title, the Biblical text, the date and place of its use. They span over forty years in time, and, in space, the entire continent. Several of them were preached from thirty to forty times, from Bowdoin College in Maine to Stanford University in California, from Vancouver to Atlanta. Some were preached three or four times in the same pulpit, of course at considerable intervals. Especially from 1910 to 1925 he was in great demand, not only in some of the big churches of the land but in academic circles; he was a regular guest preacher in a number of schools and colleges.

Most of the sermons were tapped out neatly on his own war-scarred typewriter, but few could be called "clean copy." For Dr. Vernon worked them over for different occasions; he was just as averse as anyone to sermons merely "from the barrel." The numerous hand-written comments—deleting, changing, expanding—make many pages almost illegible, but they also display a patient and meticulous workmanship which approached perfectionism.

Convinced that extempore preaching is too often an insult to a critical listener, Dr. Vernon used a full manuscript in the pulpit, marked or interlined though it might be. It was, however, no barrier between him and his congregation. His flashing eye, his tense directness and his vital concern combined to lodge his message deeply in the mind and, more importantly, in the heart and conscience of those within the reach of his voice. With such a method and manner, he never became what could be called a spell-binder or a popular preacher; but he was truly a *great* preacher, effective and deeply moving, for he always preached for a verdict to be recorded in the human heart. It was not an accident that he was called to teach the art of preaching in the Yale Divinity School and to serve as the University's chaplain.

The seventeen sermons here included were delivered by Dr. Vernon at least several times each and were therefore presumably held in high esteem by him. Also among them are those vividly remembered by friends who heard them in his active years. Every effort has been made to choose a collection truly representative of his finest homiletic work, revealing the range and variety of his interests, the height and depth of his thought, the nobility of his spirit, and the significance of his contributions to his generation.

This volume is made possible by the generosity of Dr. Vernon's niece, Miss Irmgard Kuntze. Credit for overall editorial policy and supervision of production belongs to William H. McCarter, Editor of Dartmouth Publications, and Ray Nash, Printing Adviser to the College. The heart-warming biographical sketch was written for the *Dartmouth Alumni Magazine* by one who knew Dr. Vernon from early childhood, who studied under him in Dartmouth and later taught beside him in the Department of Biography established by him, Professor Donald Bartlett.

The selecting, editing and arranging of the manuscripts has been not merely "a labor of love," but a rare experience of spiritual deepening and refreshment. To live for months in the presence of a keen mind and a great soul, through his written words, has been to renew all that is best in a precious friendship of many years duration.

Dartmouth College   ROY B. CHAMBERLIN
Hanover, New Hampshire   *Chapel Director*
October, 1955   *Professor of Religion*

AMBROSE WHITE VERNON

1870-1951

On a cold day in 1904 President Tucker of Dartmouth and his young assistant and eventual successor, Ernest Hopkins, were conversing as they walked along a Hanover path. They were discussing the installation ceremonies of Ambrose White Vernon as pastor of The Church of Christ at Dartmouth College. Mr. Hopkins, scion of a Baptist manse, asked if in the Congregational Church it was not customary for the local conference of churches to appoint a committee of their clergy to examine the new pastor in his theology. "Yes, it is customary," said President Tucker, "but in this instance it is perhaps just as well that they dispensed with it, because by the time Vernon finished with them they would have been uncertain whether the front of this church was graced with pillars or minarets."

Forty-seven years later, Dr. Vernon, Emeritus Professor of Biography at Dartmouth College, died at his home in Hanover. There lay behind him full years of preaching, lecturing, writing, teaching, and friendship throughout this country and, indeed, other countries. But Dartmouth is able to claim Dr. Vernon's resident service for more years than any other institution, whether church or college. Eleven years is the total of his active years in the faculty, and it may be symbolic that he did not in himself suggest permanence but quickening, not tradition but adventure, not acquiescence but enlistment, not circumspection nor even discretion, but rather a penetrating vision which rebuked tradition, rest or convenience. The truth—God's truth—must be searched out and proclaimed by any one aspiring to the title of Man.

In his earlier days as a Congregational minister he not only employed the scalpel of "higher criticism" in his devotion to Biblical scholarship, but he directly attacked the intellectually timid in his first book, *The Religious Values of the Old Testament*. "The greatest evil of an infallible Bible," said he, "is the worship of a trivial God." The ruthless examination to which he then subjected a Jeremiah resulted in an actual, almost

xiii

breathing Jeremiah, firmly attached to the history of his own time about which he yearned and roared. Thus the very nature of prophecy stands forth. So searching is the comprehension that the prophet is not garnished by imagination but hewn out of the solid rock of fact.

The Dartmouth of 1904 to 1907 knew Vernon as a keen competitor at tennis, as a vivid pastor of The Church of Christ, as a mountain climber, a disconcertingly honest scholar, and as a teacher of Biblical literature who was not a little inconvenient because he exhibited, invited, and exacted hard work and plenty of it.

Born in New York in 1870, Vernon studied in Morris Academy, Princeton, Union Theological Seminary, and in the Universities of Berlin, Halle, and Göttingen. Ordained in 1896, he served churches in Hiawatha, Kansas, and in East Orange, New Jersey, before coming to his Hanover pastorate and Dartmouth faculty post. From Dartmouth he moved to the professorship of Practical Theology at Yale Divinity School for two years, and then to the pastorate of the Harvard Church in Brookline, Massachusetts, where he remained from 1909 to 1918. This pastorate was remarkable for many things, none of them restful except the hospitable home which Mrs. Katherine Tappe Vernon maintained with a warmth and energy equalled only by the warmth, energy and devotion with which she criticized her husband's sermons.

A preacher who showed a sensitivity and skill to match his industry, he was also a constant and interesting pastoral caller. He had that rarest of capacities, the ability to bring comfort where it was needed, because he desired to bring comfort and because he was intelligent.

If his honesty was sometimes disconcerting, so was his change of mind when convinced, especially in those most vigorous years. Dr. Henry Sloan Coffin, with whom he edited *Hymns of the Kingdom of God*, has well said of him, "His opinions are held with zeal and tenacity, but he is open minded if you can bring him any additional light." The gadfly quality of his preaching was not its only characteristic. He exacted of himself a meticulous craftmanship, one reason for the small number of his books. But nothing could be more gracious than such sermons as the one on "Sosthenes Our Brother"—that Sosthenes who was amanuensis to the weak-eyed Paul, and helped Paul to accomplish Paul's mission in Paul's way, and earned the appellation "brother" from one of the mighty souls of history.

One would expect of such a man the intransigent liberty of conscience which was notable, but this never dimmed his loyal churchmanship. He knew that he needed, and he knew that he loved, corporate worship. This conviction never failed, nor did his love of company in sport, the theatre, music and even scholarly exploration.

The pastorate at Brookline was constructive and dynamic, but it broke upon the rocks of war with Germany. For a man who had grown from Princeton undergraduate and Union Theological student to scholar at Halle, Berlin, and Göttingen; who also had found his almost perfect complement in the lovely Harz Mountains; for a man who recognized but one master, namely Jesus, those were not good times. It is doubtful if any man ever hated tyranny and brutishness more than he, for his subsequent hatred of Hitler was Promethean. But his political loyalties in 1917 were more like those of his intimate friend Woodrow Wilson than of the Ku Klux Klan, and his solicitude for the innocent interned Germans was not always tactful in an angry society, nor, one must hazard, entirely shrewd. When the break came in 1918, of course *odium theologicum* was obtruded into the scene, and Willard Sperry is said to have remarked impatiently that here was "another instance of a heresy trial with one Christian present." This was a bitter defeat and Dr. Vernon never minimized it, but he did not dwell upon it or grow sour. He went on.

The decision to inaugurate the teaching of biography, however logical in retrospect, was not so simple as it has been told. The rare combination of scrupulous truth with vividness, coupled with the conviction that all philosophy is sterile unless wedded to human life and action, points clearly to the biographical interest. But it was not merely that biographical illustration was part of his stock in trade, for there was in him the burning conviction that there is divine purpose for human life far higher than creed or formula, if we can but find it, that there are many paths up the mountain, and that true men in their search for the truth and the heights must choose their own paths. In this he seems to have believed that Jesus himself laid such a duty upon his followers. "Wisdom is justified of all her children." It made little difference to him whether Jesus was born in Bethlehem or Nazareth, let the critical chips fall where they may. Love and the search for the Will of God was the message the Master brought to men. "Thou shalt love the Lord thy God with all thy heart and with all thy soul and with all thy mind and with all thy strength." The minds of men differ as their muscles and their finger prints, but if they are ever effective human beings they must ultimately choose a path and a purpose and cleave loyally to that commitment or they become tramps. "Biography keeps the highest crown," he said, "—a crown of thorns—for those who were progressive in spite of themselves, and not for those who took the bit in their teeth and went on to disaster. For reverence is the highest and most indispensable virtue of man." Hence we found Jeremiah, the reluctant prophet, and Paul, the erstwhile Pharisee, among his most masterly presentations, and by contrast John Brown, Alcibiades, or Mirabeau.

So it was not only a single remark of Mrs. Vernon's, nor the probably earlier suggestion of another dear friend, but the cumulation of his life that led to his latter-day venture in the teaching of biography. His mind was hot with vital conviction, the steel had long since been proven sound, and the combination of heat with the cold shock of personal defeat had put a temper in it which, with the whetting of Gamaliel Bradford's friendship, made the blade ready to cut a new path in American education. Opportunity offered in 1919 when Dr. Cowling invited him to Carleton College, and with the aid and backing of a devoted parishioner of Harvard Church he made the venture immediately significant. Students were not only excited, but they worked. They worked because Dr. Vernon made it worth while to work, and because he insisted that they make up their own minds, not sponge up "opinions." "I want you to bring me an opinion you are ready to defend."

Dartmouth was not content that Dr. Vernon should remain away from the College which had known him before and could again utilize his stimulus among the orthodox disciplines. In 1924 Dr. Vernon returned to Hanover and for eight years continued his meticulous preparations, his searching questions, his absolute silence during class debates, and the long and well-nigh illegible commentaries on every single paper, paragraph by paragraph, always asking for evidence.

After his retirement, and after much of the zest for life was lost with the death of his beloved Kätchen, Dr. Vernon's mind retained its keen temper and its refreshing ability to surprise with justice. An instance of this was the paper he wrote for Professor Wilson's "Components of Democratic Thought" in 1940, on the contribution of Christianity.

Jesus' utterances were first demonstrated not to be democratic at all. What is democratic about "I am the way, and the truth, and the life?" This was interesting from an elderly clergyman. But by the end the demonstration was even more compelling that Christianity in its primitive origin established the sacred integrity of the human soul in the minds of Western Europeans with a potency of conviction unparalleled in history. To the Greeks nonsense and to the Jews a stumbling block, but to mankind the warrant of Liberty.

Liberty demands risk, and there are many who remember his baccalaureate sermon in 1929, and they recall the very title so characteristic of the man: "The Nobler Risk." Love and truth are worth taking, nay, demand, taking risks for. One of Dr. Vernon's favorite references was to Plato's two steeds which every mortal man must harness to his chariot: the heavenly steed and the earthly. Faith and Doubt make up a risky team, but he drove them handsomely.

Any institution devoted to the enlargement of minds and the search for truth must be composed of many factors and divers personalities. Even so simple a thing as a loaf of bread has its many components. A score of institutions have been enriched and enlivened by his intellectual and spiritual vitality, but Dartmouth College has especial reason for her gratitude in the richness of the wheat and the liveliness of the yeast which Ambrose Vernon's presence supplied to her loaf of learning.

Hanover, New Hampshire   DONALD BARTLETT
November, 1951

THE NOBLER RISK

For the kingdom of heaven is as a man traveling into a far country, who called his own servants, and delivered unto them his goods. And unto one he gave five talents, to another two, and to another one; to every man according to his several ability; and straightway took his journey.

Then he that had received the five talents went and traded with the same, and made them other five talents. And likewise he that had received two, he also gained other two. But he that had received one went and digged in the earth, and hid his lord's money.

MATTHEW 25:14–18

I The Nobler Risk

The Baccalaureate, Dartmouth College, 1929

E MERSON once remarked: "People want to be settled; only so far as they are unsettled is there any hope for them." It is scarcely necessary to prove the statement that we are intellectually and spiritually in a frame of mind that would have satisfied Emerson. The doctrine of evolution, which dominates our thinking, makes us far less certain of the beginning and of the goal of creation than of the fact that it is going on. To quote another of Emerson's sentences: "Nowhere is anything final; planet, system, constellation, total nature is growing like a field of maize in July." We do not know where we have come from, where we are going, not even how we came; we only know that we are suffering change.

In particular, our religious beliefs and the intellectual presuppositions of our religion are unsettled; before such a company as this, it would be absurd not to say frankly what nearly all of us think. You have become aware that Christianity stands on a different footing now than formerly. The careful examination of the books of the Bible by Christian scholars has established the fact that those documents cannot guarantee the truth of the statements which they record. From the birth of Jesus of Nazareth we still date each revolving day, this Commencement of ours, the founding of our college and of our country and every action of our own. That he lived, that he spoke as no man ever spoke, that he died for a conviction that before him no man had harbored and that after him became the common property of the western world, that the insight of his soul has proven both the cement which has held society together and the dynamite which has blasted new paths for its progress, is assuredly true. But many of the events and utterances recorded in the Gospels, often conflicting—such as the accounts of his birth, some of the miracles, the manner of the resurrection—are now seriously questioned by multitudes of men, even professed Christians.

It would seem therefore—to men of my generation, at least—as though we once more were living in a time much like that in which Christ himself lived. It seems as if Jesus were standing in our midst and speaking for us when he declares: "The kingdom of heaven is as when a man, going into another country, called his servants and delivered unto them his goods." God as our fathers limned him, the assured message of great prophets, the faith upon which the Christian world has firmly reckoned, has left us and gone into another country. The age of paternalism, of authoritarianism, of dogmatism, has ended. The day of self-reliance, of independent thinking, of undirected stewardship, of adventure, has come.

We must remember, however, that the past has delivered unto us its goods. We are the product of our fathers' God, of our fathers' faith and struggles, of the Christian religion. No one, surely, in all the range of human history has ever so dominated the minds and hopes and ideals of men, has so formed and transformed the springs of action of the foremost peoples of the earth, as has Jesus Christ. He is largely responsible for ours. If the creeds that have been built around him have become poetic expressions of an outworn faith, we feel just as certain as Christ did, when he told this parable of the talents, that the spiritual forces of the vanishing age have left behind them their goods. They constitute the abiding ideals, the mighty hopes, the enduring values that make us men. They are our most priceless possessions. Indeed, they are what we mean when, striking beneath our bodies and minds, we come on something that we call ourselves.

And so the outstanding question which you face as you leave college and take your place in the shaping of the world is, what do you mean to do in this time of religious and spiritual uncertainty with the goods that the past has inwoven in your spirits, your ideals, your energies, your powers?

You can, of course, scorn them, jeer at them, throw them to the winds. But, fortunately, neither in Jesus' time nor in ours are there enough men of that temper to make the possibility worth considering.

There are two courses open to honest men—the same courses that Jesus pointed out in this parable to those who came to hear him in the unsettled time in which he lived. You can look on your powers and ideals as precious jewels that must be guarded anxiously against the unprincipled forces of the new age, or as tools to engage in the building of it. If they seem to you primarily jewels to be kept untarnished, you will bury them out of harm's way, as did the timid man of the parable; if you regard them as tools, you will, like the wiser servants, invest them in a large enterprise.

The counsel of Jesus, the supreme adventurer of history and therefore its supreme figure, is all in favor of this latter course. He declares in so many words that no one really possesses what he fears to lose; that "from him that hath not shall be taken away even that which he hath." This parable has made the philosophy of safety-first contemptible in the eyes of men. In its stead it has erected the most fitting philosophy of life for those who live in an obviously unsettled time like ours. It may be condensed into four words: *Take the nobler risk.* It is a slogan which Christ confirmed by his life and by his death. He affirms that if a talented man adopts it he will understand the joy of the Lord. By following it, we attain to spiritual certainty in a time of spiritual uncertainty. Decisions are demanded from us all the time on inadequate knowledge. There is always risk; we are to take the nobler one.

A great risk almost invariably fascinates us. Why should it not? Life itself is the result of a risk. We came into the world at the risk of our mothers' lives and, if they had not been willing to take the risk, we should not be here at all. We are made to love a risk, if we love human life; for human life is what happens at cost of a risk. That is fundamental; we cannot get away from it.

As Americans, also, we are the products of great risk. Ever since the time of the Greeks, people could be found who believed the world was round, but nobody would take the risk of acting on that belief. Columbus risked it. If he had wanted to save his life, he would have stayed in the court at Granada or among the looms of Genoa; he wanted, however, to do something with it, so he drummed up a crew, got on board the little caravel, pointed its pigmy bow toward the west, and America was born.

And the United States of America is the result of another risk. It was not enough to discover a new continent; it was not enough to plan a new England; this continent had to be owned by those who lived upon it. But to accomplish it a peculiarly unpromising risk had to be taken. It was so fearful that it drove Washington into rhetoric. "The once happy and peaceful plains of America," he said, "are either to be drenched with blood or inhabited by slaves. Can a virtuous man hesitate in his choice?" In Washington's eyes, safety-first meant slavery. To him but one course was open; he took the nobler risk and out of it our nation rose to life.

Nor should we pass over such an obvious confirmation of this philosophy of life as the founder of Dartmouth College. On surveying the sweep of our country and comparing it with the small patch of land that was fenced about for Moor's Charity School in Lebanon, Connecticut, he determined to risk what he had for the sake of that into which it might grow. One of the things that was uppermost in his mind was space. So he refused Albany's inducement of 2500 pounds sterling, and "the generous offers made by particular towns and parishes in the colony of Connecticut. For, the country being so filled up with inhabitants, it was not practicable to get so large a tract of lands as was thought to be most useful for it." "So, for many weighty reasons" the gentlemen of the trust in England "gave the preference to the western part of the province of New Hampshire on Connecticut river and determined that to be the place for it."

But the risk, which seems so great to us, only occasionally appalled him. Hear, again, his own words: "A little more than three years ago, there was nothing to be seen here but a horrid wilderness; now there are eleven comfortable dwelling-houses and some of them reputable ones. When I think of the great weight of present expense, I have sometimes found faintness of heart, but when I consider I have not been seeking myself in one step I have taken, nor have I taken one step without deliberation and asking counsel therein, and not only so but I have always made it my practice not to suffer my expenses to exceed what my own private interest will pay in case I should be brought to that necessity to do my creditors justice," then a dash like one of Saint Paul's and the sentence left hanging in the air, while its author lands on the great assertion: "But the consideration, which above all others has been my sovereign support, is that it is the cause of God and in him do I hope to perfect his own plan for his own glory."

That plan is still being perfected; it is not Wheelock's plan, but the risk which he took and the wholeheartedness with which he invested all he had in the enterprise are on their way to their justification. Here we sit reverently today, the product of noble risks of unselfish men; without self-stultification, we cannot turn our backs upon their policy of daring.

In all fields of human endeavor, success waits upon ventures, wholeheartedly undertaken. In military affairs, Napoleon affirms, "Death is nothing, but to live defeated and ingloriously is to die every day." In the tranquil paths of literature, Keats declares: "In Endymion I leaped headlong into the sea and thereby have become better acquainted with the soundings, the quicksands and the rocks than if I had stayed upon the green shore and piped a silly pipe and had taken tea and comfortable advice. I was never afraid of failure, for I would sooner fail than not be among the greatest." No fame without risk!

In an even higher realm, Milton is equally emphatic: "I cannot praise a fugitive and cloistered virtue, unexercised and unbreathed, that never sallies out and seeks her adversary but slinks out of the race. That which purifies us is trial, and trial is by what is contrary to us." No purity without risk!

Seeing then that society, literature, science, virtue, depend upon risks nobly taken, why is it that "safety-first" still assails our eyes from innumerable posters along the public ways? It is, alas, because men who ought to be taking noble risks insist on taking ignoble ones. "Whoever will save his life shall lose it," says Jesus. That is unequivocal and unqualified. The policy of withdrawal from conflict and danger is fatal.

But it does not therefore follow that whosoever is willing to lose his life shall save it. You must lose it *in a high enterprise* to be sure of saving it. So Jesus inserts a qualification in this half of his well-known paradox. "Whosoever loseth his life *for my sake and the gospel's* shall save it." It is only a man's ideal or his duty that can justify a great risk. To get into bed with a boy who has measles, as Mark Twain did, to sail in solitary daring across the Atlantic in a 22-foot catboat, to fly to the North Pole because no one has been there before, to overtake and pass a motor car on a curve you cannot see around—this is the kind of risk that makes safety-first posters popular and necessary.

I know of no better guide in this delicate matter than Pasteur. He refused to eat grapes without dipping them in his tumbler, in order to avoid the germs to which no duty called. But when cholera broke out in the city, he moved his desk to a room immediately above the cholera ward in the hospital, that he might better investigate the germs whose dread secrets he had set himself to conquer.

The philosophy of life that I am urging upon you by means of this parable and of human experience is not, Take any risk, but Take the nobler risk. Some risk you must take. Even the adoption of the policy of safety-first is a risk. Seeing that life demands some risk, demand of yourself that you take the nobler one. Do not simply contemplate a risk; take it.

There is a passage in a letter of William James to his mother, written when he was a senior at Harvard College, which met with sympathetic response when I read it to some of you in the classroom. It perfectly sets forth the application of our slogan to the situation you are now facing: "I feel very much the importance of making soon a final choice of my business in life. I stand now at the place where the road forks. One branch leads to material comfort, the fleshpots; but it seems a kind of selling of one's soul. The other branch leads to mental dignity and independence, combined however with physical penury. If I myself were the only one concerned, I should not hesitate an instant in my choice. On the one side is science, upon the other business (the honorable, honored and productive business of printing seems most attractive), with medicine, which partakes of advantages of both, between them, but which has drawbacks of its own. I confess, I hesitate. I fancy there is a fond maternal cowardice which would make you and every other mother contemplate with complacency the worldly fatness of a son, even if obtained by some sacrifice of his higher nature. But I fear there might be some anguish in looking back from the pinnacle of prosperity over the life you might have led in the pure pursuit of truth. It seems as if one could not afford to give that up for any bribe, however great."

Because William James took what seemed to him the nobler risk, hundreds of intelligent men have run the race of life with a rationally fortified religious faith. Safety-first at the crossways where James found himself and where you are finding yourselves is intellectual and spiritual suicide. If you choose to save your life there, you may make money and achieve comfort and position, but life will slip through your fingers. If you choose to lose your life in a great enterprise that arouses your manhood, you will save it.

It is my deliberate opinion that if your own soul permits you to adopt as your life slogan, "Take the nobler risk," the great problem of religion which confronts us all in this time of confusion will be at once settled.

No one has ever seen God or can tell you what he is or altogether how he works or quite what he means to do with us. In fact, we are all of us poignantly aware that no one can demonstrate that there is a God at all. Science and philosophy leave the way open for religion and all the deeper experiences of men call for it, but, as the Bible has long ago assured us, without *faith* it is impossible to please God or even to reach him. And faith implies facing the greatest of all risks and taking it. You must live either as though there were God, a great constraining power, making for a noble end and bound to reach it, or else as though there were no such directive, cooperative principle in the universe and that life therefore has no high and sacred meaning.

Now, if what I have been saying seems to you true, if the manly fashion of living is to take a noble risk rather than to await a never-dawning certainty, then there can be no question of the risk that we should take. It is far nobler to take the religious risk than to take the irreligious one. Then take it. And if we take it, we shall take it as followers of Christ. I do not mean that we shall regard him as the second person of a mysterious deity. I mean that our attitude to God—to the inscrutable power that has produced, quickened, empowered and guided our life—should be so full of childlike trust and gratitude that the way of love shall become our way of life.

That is the supreme risk—to live not for comfort or for fame but for service, to shut the door upon thoughts of self and open it upon your fellows; to spend yourself loyally for the institutions which make for brotherhood and truth in the world; to refuse to defend yourself or to let a friend go undefended; to bear suffering rather than inflict it; to outlaw every grudge; to spend more thought on giving than on receiving, on knowing than on getting known; to recognize money and time as sacred trusts rather than as private playthings; to reject any plan which permanently withdraws you from human service for the sake of personal pleasure; to take your stand definitely with the oppressed rather than with the oppressors, with the ostracized rather than with the exclusive, but to be prepared to serve them both; to let humor have the right of way over pride but to hush it in the presence of earnest thought or deep sorrow; to be friendly, if possible even toward the bigoted and the cynical and the snobbish; to put your character at the disposal of love as utterly as marble is placed under the chisel of the sculptor—this, fellow-students, fellow men of Dartmouth, fellow seekers after God, is taking the supreme risk.

No matter how sincerely, how wholeheartedly you take it, it will never lose its element of risk, of venture, of heroism; but the longer and the more consistently you take it, the more confident you will become that you have sailed a straight course in a time of uncertainty.

There is a stanza of a comparatively obscure English poet with which I shall close this address you have asked me to give. It owes its growing favor solely to its simple and important truth:

> "To every man there openeth
> A way and ways and a way,
> And the high soul climbs the high way
> And the low soul gropes the low;
> And in between on the misty flats,
> The rest drift to and fro.
> But to every man a high way and a low,
> And every man decideth the way his soul shall go."

I THOUGHT THAT I OUGHT

I *verily* thought *with myself,* that I ought *to do many things contrary to the name of Jesus of Nazareth* . . . *and many of the saints did I shut up in prison* . . . *and when they were put to death, I gave my voice against them.*

ACTS 26:9–10

II "I Thought That I Ought"

WHAT a tragedy Paul depicts in these words! The passage, in the midst of his defense before King Agrippa, is a brief description of his life as an orthodox Jew. His subsequent conversion on the road to Damascus did not bring his victims out of the grave, for so far as they were concerned the tragedy was over. "I thought that I ought" may excuse the tragedy, but it could not annul it. It could not for Paul; it cannot for any one of us. And it seems to me that nowhere is the limitation of our humanity more apparent than when we survey the misery or desolation resulting from deeds we thought we ought to do. We dare not say that we ought not to have followed the ought. But with Paul we grow uncertain about the moral deliverance, and say, apologetically rather than defiantly, "Well, I thought that I ought."

It is fair to note, however, that there is a genuine crumb of personal comfort in remembering that some of the noblest men are in our company. "Zeal for God, but not according to knowledge," Paul tells us was the typical attitude of the Jewish race; here, too, he confesses that it was his own. Luther thought he ought to sanction the bigamy of Philip of Hesse. Calvin thought Servetus ought to be burned. The Church of Rome thought it ought to establish the inquisition. The early Protestants and the Catholics thought they ought to slay 2000 Anabaptists who freed religion from bondage to the state. The Episcopalians thought they ought to murder three of the original Congregationalists of England and drive the rest into exile. The Puritans of Massachusetts Bay thought they ought to banish Roger Williams, to kill Quakers and to withhold civic franchise from all who did not agree with *their* conception of the Christian faith.

Some of the most frightful deeds recorded in history were done because the perpetrators thought that they ought. That does not prove them to be men of abnormally low moral insight; they thought they were serving God—but "without knowledge," as Paul reminds us. Jesus' prayer, "Father, forgive them, for they know not what they do," is a prayer that he must pray not only over his bitterest enemies, but also over many of his most devoted followers. The terrifying evils of asceticism, of idolatry, of superstition, have been usually set in action not by sinners, but by saints.

Though this consideration may keep us back from extreme personal self-condemnation, it does not relieve us from the responsibility of wrecking human happiness by not doing what we think we ought. And so I would like to make some simple suggestions that, if followed, might restrain us from piling up that wreckage.

First, when the urgent necessity comes upon us of entering a course of action which carries with it the possibility of distress for others, let us be sure that we are making sufficient allowance for other people's ought. Our ought is no more sacred to us than theirs to them. Ever conscious of our own ignorance and waywardness, we must admit the possibility that their ought may be even more enlightened than ours; it is certainly as binding.

That was what Paul forgot, thus bringing unending remorse into his own soul and irretrievable suffering to many others. He forgot that no man, no matter how "righteous" or sincere, has a right to attempt to force his convictions upon others. He forgot how truly ignorant all men are in the light of God's wisdom, for he had not yet reached the high level of spiritual insight revealed in his immortal 13th chapter of First Corinthians, "For we know *in part*," and only in part. And it is high time for all who wear the name of Christian to finish with all such suspicion, intolerance, cruelty, and all bigotry in the name of religion, and deliberately to cultivate that spirit of meekness which is so supposedly unmanly but so essentially Christian.

Again, doing what we think we ought often brings great misery to ourselves and others because we forget our own liability to error. Whatever we ought or ought not to do, we ought to remember that there are wiser and better people in the world than we, with whom we should take counsel. Paul says in our text, "I thought *with myself* that I ought." When people think with themselves, their ought is apt to be unduly diluted by too much of themselves. When you confront a crisis in your life, and think that you ought, for example, to turn your back on the most precious hopes of your parents for you, or to change the policy of your business, or expose your loved ones to a serious danger, before you do what you think you ought, do what you *know* you ought and consult the wisest and most Christlike souls you know, not simply for confirmation of your own conviction but for reverent enlightenment of your own soul.

And doing what we think we ought often brings us to Paul's regret, because we forget the mighty force of our habits, our prejudices, our traditions. Paul persecuted the Christians before he understood them. Since they transgressed his holiest convictions, they must be silenced. Who can tell how many salutary and redeeming ideas have been lost to mankind because they have been suppressed before they were examined! Here we often overlook one of Jesus' own utterances, "Take heed how ye hear, for to him that hath shall be given." We have stupidly maintained that he meant that we should guard against opening our ears to the evil, whereas it is quite clear from the second clause of his command that he was warning us against *not* opening our ears to the good, because it was strange. "Whoso hath ears, let him hear," he exclaimed.

But we are always driven back to the ought. We must beware lest we mistake the ought for our own overmastering desire. We must safeguard others' ought from the unconsidered ought of our own. We must take noble counsel at crises. We must be on our watch against the subtle powers of tradition and prejudice. But we must not let caution and wisdom usurp the mighty rights of the ought. "I thought that I ought" is a far better slogan than the far commoner one, "I thought I couldn't." The desolation that a conscientious man sometimes unnecessarily spreads about him is less offensive to God and less obstructive to his Kingdom than the sluggishness of all human motive that ensues upon the dethronement of conscience. Mistakes at this point are tragic, but whether we make them or not we must do what we think we ought. The ought never fails to summon us.

And here our text suggests an even greater comfort than any I have mentioned. Because Paul did what he thought he ought, he never actually departed from God. Though he persecuted the righteous and slew the innocent, he kept his conscience pure and therefore his heart was open to illumination from above. And that illumination came. On the road to Damascus, the man who thought that he ought discovered *what* he ought. And then he did not hesitate to break with his past in order that he might not break with his ought. Because he had never really broken with his ought, God, to whom he looked up blindly, used him as he has been able to use few others for the permanent establishment of his Kingdom among men.

It is curious how little is said in that Damascus experience about sin and forgiveness. There was a mighty conversion, a man whose life direction was totally reversed, but as a matter of fact he had simply found the one road for which he had long been searching. To do what one thinks one ought is the best way to discover what one really ought. "If a man willeth to do the will of God, he shall know of the doctrine." Between the willing and the knowing there may be a long road, a road of confusion and even of brutality and bloodshed, but upon the honest and devoted soul that walks it a light will arise at some blessed noonday above the brightness of the sun. Since Paul never forfeited his devotion to God's will as he understood it, the murderer for conscience' sake was redeemed. The bitterest and ablest persecutor of Christianity was enabled to share in it, with shame to be sure but with a boundless gratitude.

An awareness of the disasters of our own shortsightedness and of the injuries we have visited upon others because "we thought we ought" leads me to another and most important suggestion, for it confronts us with the very heart of the Gospel—the mystery of God's love. It is not only the man who does what he thinks he ought and blunders in doing it that God reconciles to Himself and takes anew in His service; it is also the man who does what he thinks he ought not. There is a certain grandeur about the disasters that befall mankind when they are the outcome of a sense of duty, for often nobility of character outbalances the frightful errors of reason. But the wilful disregard of the holiest within us seems unforgivable indeed. We feel that God's restrained wrath must burst forth over the heads of those who deliberately march to their own pleasure over the pain they purposely inflict upon His children. Not mere blunderers, but sinners; not those who hurt others for conscience' sake, but those who do so for their own low gratifications! But oh, my friends, here is the measureless mystery and consolation of the Gospel.

The younger and wandering son, in the parable read to us today, did not do what he thought he ought when he took the portion of goods that fell to him, went to the far country and there wasted his father's substance in riotous living. He did what he *knew* that he ought not. But it was not the selfish, contemptible fellow from the swine-field that the father saw in the dim distance trudging toward home, but the repentant son upon whom he had compassion, to whom he ran and for whom he brought the best robe and killed the fatted calf.

And it is because of that parable and of the experience therein portrayed that most of us are now in the Father's service. It is not because of the ought that we truly live, but because of love. Through the love of God the ought has become reestablished in our lives; for the love does not depend upon the ought, but the ought upon the love. The ought wobbles, but not the love of God! We know we cannot drift beyond His love and care.

And so, my friends, let none of us ever mistake the proclamation of righteousness for the proclamation of the Gospel. Let the silences of our souls be filled with God's love. Righteousness, in any strict sense, may be impossible to us. Wisdom is certainly beyond our reach most of the time. Only too often we fail in goodness and kindness. Let us at least not fail in keeping our hearts so continually open to the love of God that it may flow through us unto all the world. To love God with all the heart and mind and soul, and to love our fellowmen on that account, this is quite within the reach of all of us. The failure is the most inexcusable of all sins, but the love of God is not balked even by that.

THE SECRET OF SUCCESS

Whosoever will save his life shall lose it, and whosoever will lose his life for my sake shall find it.

MARK 8:35

III The Secret of Success in Life

A Vesper Talk

AT the very outset, my friends, I take for granted two things: first, that Jesus of Nazareth has shown us the highest type of life; and, second, that it is our business to make our lives of the highest type, rather than either of the lowest or of a type somewhere between the highest and the lowest. On that basis I wish to speak to you on the secret of success in human life. This, you say, is a large theme for twelve minutes. It is just that, but the secret is not hard to find if we start from this text.

For, you see, there are simply two principles of supreme importance which, taken together, put success in our hands and give us the crowning satisfactions in life. The first is that selfishness of any kind is fatal. If some one had come to us and had asked us how to make a success out of life, we should certainly have been inclined to tell him: don't waste it; see what talents you have and develop them; be industrious, honest, determined; and thus you will get the best the world has to offer. But that is not Jesus' idea at all. He says, rather, if a man *sets out* to save his life he is bound to lose it. That is, if he puts prudence in charge of his career, it is sure to be a small and a rather mean one.

There is a splendid illustration of this in a verse from one of the oldest poems in the Bible, the Song of Deborah, in the fifth chapter of Judges. You remember that shortly after the Israelites had entered Palestine, they scattered and soon became almost slaves of the more powerful Canaanites, and things came to such a pass that it became evident that, if they were to survive at all, there must be a decisive battle fought. If the tribes fought singly, they were certain to lose, so messengers were despatched bidding each one to contribute contingents to the great army that was to be gathered under Barak.

But when the battle was fought and won, Reuben, a tribe settled east of the River Jordan, had sent no company to aid his brothers. The poet who described the victory pillories Reuben in these suggestive words:

> By the watercourses of Reuben, there were great
>   searchings of hearts.
> Why satest thou among the sheepfolds, to hear the
>   pipings of the flocks?

You see, Reuben saved his life and avoided the risks of combat. When the trumpet called, instead of listening to it, he listened to the pipings of the flocks. He refused to leave what he had for the sake of his distressed brothers. He made a great decision in a self-regardful mood, and so he lost the power and joy of a great conquest.

And it is always so. You remember that a rich young ruler came to Jesus one day and asked him how he might live the highest life. And Jesus told him that he must sell his possessions and come and follow him. But the young man couldn't tear himself from his wealth; probably he had never enjoyed a higher pleasure than counting his interest. In any case, he lost the exultation of that small body of Christians who changed the whole face of the world.

It is so even on a higher level. If a man is always thinking how to keep his soul unspotted from the world, he gets to be a mean man, a disagreeable man, a kill-joy. "Whosoever," says Jesus, "will save his life shall lose it"—whether it is a lustful life, or an intellectual life, or a spiritual life. No man *must* live. If your aim is to get the most out of life, you will get very little. "What will you give me?" is a question which, if accepted as a motto, ruins any life. That was the question on Judas' lips, you remember, as he sold his Lord. Don't get your life tuned to that; if you do, you have already lost all the best things in life.

Another question and its answer lead us to the second principle of successful living. If we are not to try to save our lives, what are we going to lose them for?

There are many ways in which you can lose your life or, as we should say, throw our lives away. Here, for instance, is a man who, having failed in business, hurls himself under a moving locomotive or blows his brains out. How fearful! we say. He has been guilty of blasphemy; he has laid his hands on a life that God had given him, and has sacrificed it to his distorted pride.

And here is another man who throws his life away in drinking and gambling. He lives ten years less than his allotted span of years, and each is an ignoble one. His parents hang their heads in shame because he is throwing a sacred life away as plainly as if he had cast it before a locomotive.

Another man, in the prime of life, sees a canoe overturned in the river and, being a strong swimmer, strikes out to save his fellow. But the current sweeps him to his death. The grieving parents, however, do not hang their heads for him. His name is on every lip and the Church holds his memory sacred. But did not he also throw away a life that God had given him? Yes, he did; but it may be that God meant him to.

And here is still another. He is a clerk in a store in the business day, and in the evening goes about as an agent for a book concern. His friends are anxious for him, his physician warns him that he is killing himself, and he fears that they speak the truth. He can see in the glass that his cheeks are growing pale and sunken; he feels too that his energy is gone and that he does not have as good luck with his customers as he did. But he goes on day after day, and at last a slight illness overtakes him and he has no strength to withstand it. With a weary smile he says for the last time, "Our Father who art in heaven," and passes away. Was not he also wicked to abuse the life that God had lent him? Wicked? He had a crippled wife, an aging mother, and four children in school, and he was their only support. It may be possible that God meant him to work himself to death.

And if I were to speak of a fifth, I could not omit the greatest of all, who gave his life as a ransom for many, whose life no man took from him, but who laid it down of himself. I am sure you see what I mean and what Jesus meant in this text. The way to save your life, to get the most of life, is to throw it away *in a great cause*; that is the noblest thing a man can do, and it is certainly the largest. For if you are living for yourself, *you* are the biggest thing you know. But if you are living for some great cause, you have found something far bigger. You have escaped into the larger life.

You see, therefore, that the clear way to success in human living is to find some great cause dearer to you than life itself, and throw yourself away for it. It must be large to justify so great a sacrifice, but it is your business to find it. And Jesus gives you a broad hint when he says, "Whosoever loses his life *for my sake,* the same shall save it." To live for him justifies you in sacrificing your life. It gives a height and breadth to life that I see no other way to get. It gives you God to trust, and the Kingdom of God to work for night and day. The supreme business of every man, then, is to love Jesus Christ.

And so we have our two principles which together constitute the secret of success in human life. The first one is that selfishness is always fatal, no matter how low or high a life may be. And the second principle is that if a man is to live abundantly he must find a cause so high, so large, so holy, that for it, in the sight of God, he has a right to throw away the life that God had given him. And Jesus can show him such a cause, and therefore he can be his redeemer.

RESIST EVIL

Whosoever smiteth thee on thy right cheek, turn to him the other also.

MATTHEW 5:30

IV When May We Resist Evil?

THIS unequivocal statement, with a few others in the same vein, has been perhaps the most difficult of Jesus' specific teachings for his would-be followers to understand fully and to apply honestly. It presents them with a peculiar moral paradox, acute particularly in time of "war and rumors of war." When we reluctantly entered the colossal war from which we have just emerged, we did not turn to our New Testaments to see if we should do so, but to our hearts. We believe that we did right in so doing, and that we showed that we did not live by the letter, but by the spirit, the ultimate authority for those who believe in a living God.

For all that, any Christian who diverges from the counsels of Jesus does so only with greatest hesitation. And this teaching of his which forms our text today is no incidental remark. He was aware that by it he was reversing some of the sacred habits of the race. We feel that it is a peculiarly characteristic manifestation of his spirit. Must one, who believes that a world war, with all its barbarities and tragedy, must be waged and won, draw away a considerable distance from him who said it?

Superficially, it does seem necessary. It has been reported that some people who circulated printed copies of the Sermon on the Mount among British troops were put in prison. Would it not be curious indeed if we found ourselves most convinced of the sublimity of our ideals at the moment when we seemed to contradict the Man who had most to do with making them sublime? Must we accept this anomaly in morals? Perhaps we'd better seek to understand this vital saying before we reject it.

Fortunately, two of the most influential men of the past century have given us notable interpretations of the text. They are very diverse and, if we attend to them both, I think that we should expect some light.

One of them consciously attempted to Christianize what he regarded as a faithless generation by emphasizing this precept of our Lord. I refer, of course, to Tolstoi, and I lay before you some characteristic words of his which contain his understanding of the text—an interpretation, by the way, which infuriated the Russian Orthodox Church, amazed the government, and sent a thrill of hope through the hearts of the people.

"As a man cannot lift a mountain and as a kindly man cannot kill an infant, so a man living the Christian life cannot take part in deeds of violence. How is a man to act when he sees a robber killing or outraging a child? Who shall say that the child's life is more needed, is better, than the robber's? To decide that, he needs to know what would become of the child he saves, and what—had he not killed him—would have been the future of the robber he kills.

"And as he cannot know this, the non-Christian has no rationally sufficient ground for killing the robber. But if a man is a Christian, and consequently acknowledges God and sees the meaning of life in fulfilling His will, then, however ferocious the robber, however innocent and lovely the child, he has even less ground to abandon the God-given law and to do to the robber what the robber wishes to do to the child. He may plead with the robber, may interpose his own body between the robber and the victim, but there is one thing he cannot do: he cannot deliberately abandon the law he has received from God, the fulfilment of which alone gives meaning to life."

And Tolstoi has the courage not to shrink from the consequences of such an interpretation. He will not countenance violence in any sphere. He will not concede to the state what he denies to the individual. As all governments are founded on the principle of violence toward the law-breaker, which he repudiates, he says:

"A man should, first of all, neither willingly nor under compulsion, take any part in governmental activity, and should therefore be neither a soldier, nor a tax-collector, nor a juryman, nor a Member of Parliament, nor in fact hold any office connected with violence. That is one thing.

"Secondly, a man should not voluntarily pay taxes to governments, nor should he accept money collected by taxes either as salary or as pension or as reward, nor make use of governmental institutions supported by taxes collected from the people by violence.

"Thirdly, he should not appeal to governmental violence for the protection of his possessions in land nor in other things, but should only possess land and the product of his toil in so far as others do not claim them from him."

Here, my friends, we have the revival, by a man of great genius, of the theory which in somewhat milder form produced that fascinating historical movement in which the names of Fox and William Penn have become immortal, the Society of Friends. Through it men have been forced once more to consider our text and to weigh afresh their own allegiance to its spirit. It is not necessary for us to discuss this theory at length for, whatever may be its own merits and defects, it is clearly mistaken as an explanation of the meaning of the words with which we are concerned today. For we need only to recall the familiar words, "Render to Caesar the things that are Caesar's," to assure ourselves at once that Tolstoi's mind at this point is not the mind of our Lord.

The fact, however, that this particular interpretation is wrong does not give us any excuse for going on our belligerent way as though Jesus had said, "Whosoever smiteth thee on the right cheek, be sure to smite his in return." Is there any other explanation which is in accord with the great body of Christ's teachings and which can justify us in the hope that in it we may find some principle of living which we may build into the very foundations of our lives? That is a question which no earnest disciple of Jesus may evade.

I believe that a greater man than Tolstoi, no less a man than Abraham Lincoln, has given us, in deed as well as in word, such an interpretation. No President of the United States ever had so many of his own party smite him on the cheek. He was almost unanimously belittled by the members of his own cabinet. Seward, you remember, gave up a trip to Europe because he thought that the safety of the country depended upon his presence, rather than on the judgment of the vulgar western backwoodsman. Others around his cabinet table merely tolerated him, thinking they could use him for their own ends. But Lincoln knew that his business was not to make men respect him, but rather to hold together the forces that loved the Union. So he suffered this contempt; he turned the other cheek.

A friend came to him one day and said, "I have positive evidence that Mr. Chase is plotting on a large scale to win the next convention for himself and to succeed you in the Presidency, and it is high time that you dismiss him." But Lincoln simply responded, "I have determined to shut my eyes as far as possible to everything of that sort. Mr. Chase makes a good Secretary, and I shall keep him where he is. If he becomes President, all right. I hope that we shall never have a worse one." That is an eminently practical interpretation of the words we are considering. Here Lincoln turned the other cheek. And to turn the other cheek to a noble man is much harder than to turn it to an insignificant one.

Of all the men with whom Lincoln had to deal, there was perhaps no one who possessed more ability, was more indispensable to his country, was more devoted to duty, or had a greater disdain for the President, than one of his leading generals. Lincoln thought more of the first characteristics than of the last, and treated him therefore with greatest consideration. Once, for example, he waived his rights as Commander-in-Chief and, instead of summoning McClellan from the camp near Washington to the White House, he went to the headquarters to consult with him. When he arrived the general was out. The President went into the little reception room and waited patiently. After a while he heard the steps of someone entering the house and ascending the stairs, and then silence. Shortly the orderly came to the President and reported that the general had gone to his room, being too tired to see his Commander-in-Chief. What did Lincoln say? He said nothing!

In one of the dark hours of the war Lincoln thought it his duty to appoint General Hooker as the commanding officer of the Union Army. The President's closest friends were rebellious, saying, "Don't you know that Hooker has been deriding you publicly for months? Why should you appoint him to the most important and responsible position in your gift?" "Because," he replied, "he stands highest with the country and commands the people's confidence as no other man. It makes no difference what he says about me." His whole public action recalls what he said on another occasion: "What I deal with is too vast for malicious dealings."

As we recall these typical refusals to strike back, let us not forget that Lincoln had gained his first reputation as the champion wrestler and prize fighter of his rough frontier region. This fact prepares us for what may be regarded as almost a commentary on our text, a letter addressed to an officer in active service who had been court-martialed for quarreling:

"My dear Sir: The advice of a father to his son was, 'Beware of entrance to a quarrel, but, being in, see to it that the opponent may beware of thee,' is good but not the best. Quarrel not at all. No man, resolved to make the most of himself, can spare time for personal contention, including the vitiating of his temper, and his loss of self-control. Yield larger things to which you can show no more than equal right, and yield lesser ones though clearly your own. Better give your path to a dog than be bitten by him in contesting the road. Even killing the dog would not cure the bite."

With this living interpretation of Lincoln and the somewhat speculative one of Tolstoi in mind, let us ask ourselves if we cannot find in Christ's own life incidents that will assure us of what he meant and of what he did not mean when he proclaimed, If a man smite thee on the right cheek, turn to him the other also.

Immediately we recall that great moment when Jesus stood before Pilate, the Roman governor of Palestine. Facing him were the venomous priests and scribes hurling forth their charges of sedition and blasphemy. And Jesus—answered nothing. Whereupon the governor marveled and called upon him, "Hearest thou not how many things they accuse thee of?" And Jesus answered nothing. It is even recorded that one who stood by literally smote him upon the face. He smote not in return but said, "If I have spoken evil, bear witness of the evil; if well, why smitest thou me?" Our Lord took his own counsel seriously in the deciding moment of his career; it behooves us to take it seriously also.

But even as we marvel with Pilate at the serenity with which he took personal insult, there comes to our mind that act of our Lord that was to some extent responsible for his standing before the governor at all.

We see him approaching Jerusalem, perhaps for the first time since he was a boy. He rides through its storied streets with the palms and robes strewn upon his way and with the hallelujahs resounding from the walls of the houses, until he reaches the sacred Temple. We see him reverently dismounting, ascending the steps, finding the money-changers and the sellers of doves and animals, and the people haggling over money in the holy place. We see the color rising in his cheeks; we feel the depth of his indignation; we behold him driving that mob of merchants single-handed from their tables and their gold. And no one of that company would have maintained with Tolstoi that the Man of Nazareth did not believe in violence.

How then shall we express in a sentence the mind of our Lord on the resistance of evil? May we not put it thus? If a man strikes *you*, do not strike back; if a man strikes your *ideal*, then out with the whip!

We take it for granted that no man of earnest soul will have an ideal without thereby at the same time having a purpose, the purpose, namely, of defending that ideal to the uttermost. An ideal is not an idea; it is a great moral reality. And the ideal is not created by the man who cherishes it; in the moral realm, in the realm of his personality, it creates him, or it shatters him.

Here is a creature of flesh and blood and affection and brain like other beasts. And into the midst of him there marches unawares an ideal, takes possession of his faculties, organizes his forces, cuts loose the sinew that binds him to the earth, makes him a man. If he is to remain a man, if there is to be in him something not of this world, something that makes him smile at the stars and disarm supercilious Death, then he must see in that ideal the meaning of his life. His purpose must be to keep it unspotted from the world. For it he must count his life dear, but chiefly for it; his life must not be dear unto himself.

Every man then who has an ideal has a purpose. If we bear this in mind, I think we shall recognize that through this forgotten plank of the Christian platform we have come upon one of the great principles of the Christian religion. We may state it as we have already: "If a man smite thee upon the cheek, turn to him the other; if a man smite your ideal, out with the whip!" Or we may state it thus—and it is the same thing: "It is a man's purpose that is sacred, not his person."

This is what Lincoln felt as he suffered indignity to himself rather than imperil his purpose of keeping together in one united body all who loved the Union. This must have been what our Lord meant when he said, "If a man speak a word against the Son of Man, it shall be forgiven him, but if he shall speak against the Holy Spirit (that which inspires and drives and sanctifies my life), it shall never be forgiven him, neither in this world nor in that which is to come."

This is what Clough meant in his vivid poem *Dipsychus*. Some of you, I hope, are familiar with it and remember how its hero, upon being insulted on the street, thus answered the demand that he defend his honor:

> "To bleed for others' wrongs
> In vindication of a cause,
> The sword of the Lord and Gideon—Oh, that seems
> The flower and top of life! But fight because
> Some poor misconstruing trifler haps to say
> I lie, when I do not lie,
> Why should I? Call you this a cause? I can't.
> Oh, he is wrong, no doubt; he misbehaves—
> But is it worth so much as speaking loud?
> And things so merely personal to myself
> Of all earth's things do least affect myself."

And so these words which we have been considering today help us to great convictions. First, if I am sensitive concerning my rights and my honor and my person, than I am a small man, because I am not in the grip of an overmastering purpose. The man who strikes back when his cheek is struck is a small man who, having nothing sacred to defend, defends the dearest thing he has, his own person.

Secondly, the follower of Jesus Christ is bound, by all the sacredness of Passion Week which began with a whip of small cords and ended with the silence before Pilate, to be in possession of a purpose which relieves him from preoccupation with his own person and cheapens his honor, as it did for his Lord. We must care less for the immortality of our souls than for the immortality of the purpose to which we have devoted our lives. We must be careless about face scratches because we are engaged in bringing in the Kingdom of God. A brave soldier thinks not about defending his life but about winning his battle.

Therefore we are called upon to resist evil, not when it stings us, but only when it besmirches our ideal and threatens our purpose. Each of us has two priceless rights: the right to defend his fellow-man, and the right not to defend himself. The one makes him chivalrous, and the other makes him free.

PLAY THE MAN

And he said, If the Syrians be too strong for me, then thou shalt help me: but if . . . Ammon be too strong for thee, then I will come and help thee. Be of good courage, and let us play the man *for our people, and for the cities of our God:* and the Lord do that which seemeth him good.

II SAMUEL 10:11–12

V "Let Us Play the Man"

A Dartmouth College Vesper Sermon

MOST efficient commanders in the wars of the world, I presume, have actually typified the fundamental convictions of the armies which they have led. Men who fall below the average level of thought and action of the men they lead cannot set going their unused higher resources. Nor, on the other hand, can leaders too much in advance of their men make sufficient connection with them to win their confidence; however far behind the battle-line the commanding general is obliged to place his person, his mind should be within sight of the army and yet a little ahead of it. He should be a high and passionate representative of the men he leads.

Every once in a while in some great campaign, the tension of war is so great that it seems to compress the personality of a competent commander into a single sentence. And when he is a true representative of his nation, this sentence flashes upon us a new understanding of the national character and ambition. Take, for example, the famous order that the flags of Nelson's fleet fluttered through the air at the battle of Trafalgar, "England expects every man to do his duty." More than hundreds of learned treatises, that command reveals to us the doggedness and determination and intrepidity of the British. When Napoleon led his dashing army to battle under the pyramids of Egypt and called out, "Men, forty centuries look down on you," we feel ourselves stirred by the knightly ambitions and the thirst of fame that have been at the heart of France, the chivalrous and the idealistic. And much as the American people were moved with pride by the victory of their fleet over the Spaniards off the Cuban coast, dearer to some than even the victory was the immortal command of Admiral Philip subduing the exultant cheers of his victorious sailors, "Don't cheer, men; they're dying." Through that command we come upon a tenderness and magnanimity that lie deep in the heart of the American democracy.

And the words which I have chosen for our text today belong, I think, in this group of war-orders which reveal the heart of great nations. The words were uttered by Joab, one of the most bloodthirsty and yet at the same time one of the most loyal of the ancient Israelites, the prop of David's throne. They came from his lips at a great crisis, when Ammon had persuaded Syria to join her in a coalition against Israel. Joab divided his outnumbered troops into two divisions and, appointing his brother Abishai as leader of one, gave him his orders, "Be of good courage and . . . play the man . . . ; and the Lord do that which seemeth him good." In this battle-order there is compressed the temper of that peculiar people through whom alone God was able adequately to interpret his ways to men. It reveals, in proper conjunction, two indispensable qualities of the highest manhood. Let us consider them together today.

First is "playing the man." It is a great phrase and, as the centuries since it was uttered have come and gone, it has echoed and reechoed and has never been lost. And whenever it has been used, it has meant much the same thing as when Joab first used it fighting the forgotten nations of the Near East, then so threatening. He meant by "playing the man" what we mean by it, putting all our force behind our highest possessions, risking all for the defense of those dearest and noblest things which we do *not* share with all the world, realizing that just because we are men we are dedicated to the defense and to the glorification and to the eventual triumph of our ideal.

It was of course quite true that our ideal and Joab's are not identical. Israel was his ideal; it was for that particular people of his that he determined to play the man. America is our people, perhaps no nobler a nation but a richer and larger one. Underneath America is Liberty, and underneath Liberty is respect and love for our neighbor. The ideal of Joab and the ideal of a twentieth-century American Christian are of course not the same, and that wherein they differ is of most priceless worth, but I repeat that to play the man is essentially the same for Joab and for us.

It is to put at the service of our highest and best all we possess. Playing the man, therefore, does not depend so much upon what we regard as our highest as it depends upon what we are prepared to risk for its sake. Possessions of the spirit are not in our power to accumulate; they are bestowed upon us by our God in marvelous ways, treasures for which we would lay down our lives, treasures for the sake of which we mean to live out our lives. To play the man means to regard ourselves as their defenders, no matter what comes.

When the prophet Amos, for example, realized that the Lord demanded righteousness rather than sacrifice, he did not inquire as to the feasibility of saying so. "The lion hath roared," he declared, "who doth not tremble with fear?" There is no question about the trembling. "When the Lord speaks who can but utter his message"—that is likewise inevitable for the man who has heard it.

The early Christians, hounded by their fellows, persecuted through all countries and betrayed by all sort of folk, never dreamed that Christianity was practical. They supposed, indeed, that it was meant for another world which God would prepare for them, and just because they were intent upon that world they conquered this. Paul was martyred and so was Peter, but the New Testament does not mention their deaths; martyrdom was too frequent to be regarded as notable.

John Brown was a visionary or a fanatic, but because he put himself utterly at the service of his ideal, he was useful. Just before his death he wrote his brother in a postscript to a business letter: "I am quite cheerful in view of my approaching end, being fully persuaded that I am worth inconceivably more to hang than for any other purpose."

And when Jesus saw the Cross ahead, he refused to alter his course or his faith or his message. There he proved his manhood. The question that underlies manhood is not primarily one of wisdom, or what do you believe and how far does it tally with the beliefs of others. It is a matter of loyalty. How far are you prepared to go in manifesting and defending your ideal, be that ideal what God pleases?

Recall the noble words of President Wilson at the Brooklyn Navy Yard, after Secretary Daniels had presented him a roll of the men who had fallen at Vera Cruz:

"War, gentlemen, is only a sort of dramatic representation of a thousand forms of duty. I never went into battle, I was never under fire, but I fancy there are some things just as hard to do as to go under fire. I fancy that it is just as hard to do your duty when men are jeering at you as when they are shooting at you. When they shoot at you, they can only take your natural life; when they sneer at you, they can wound your heart.

"So when I look at you, I feel as if I also, and we all, were enlisted men. Not enlisted in your particular branch of the service, but enlisted to serve the country, no matter what may come, what though we may waste our lives in the arduous endeavor. We are expected to put the utmost energy of every power that we have into the service of our fellow-men, never sparing ourselves, not condescending to think of what is going to happen to ourselves, but ready, if need be, to go to the utter length of complete self-sacrifice."

The first basic principle of manhood, to play the man, needs a second principle to complete and to deepen it. When Joab told Abishai to play the man, he did not assure him of victory, as most commanders are wont to do. He did not say, "Be of good courage and let us play the man . . . and we shall surely win." Most of us, had we been in Joab's place, would, I suppose, have said that, whether we believed it or not. For men can fight better who are assured of triumph; it is indeed that sense of triumph that commanders are supposed to give.

But Joab's command did not run that way. "Let us play the man . . . and let the Lord do that which seemeth him good." He was not attempting to force God's hand; he was not fighting primarily to gain a victory, but to do his duty. He and Abishai were to play the man not for their triumph but for God's. The Lord was to do with their fighting and their persons and their ambitions and their people what seemed to him good. Their God was too mysterious to be assured that, even when they played the man, they could understand his purpose. They might be altogether wrong in their judgment; but God would not let their false judgment block his; they were offering to God a definite exhibition of loyalty for him to use as he would. They would do their duty, and he would accept their service even though he would perhaps utterly transform it.

Here, my friend, is where many of us may still learn important lessons from this barbarian commander. We think we know God so well, and understand his modes of action and his will concerning the children of men so completely, that we cannot be defeated if we fight our best under the banner of Christ. And there is no doubt that we *do* know far more of God than did Joab, and that the time-tested customs of our Christian society do represent sacred channels of the divine life. But we do not sit on the throne of God when we play the man; we are not defending the whole truth when we defend our ideal; the Truth is too sublime for us to see. Like Joab, we are only giving God, by our loyalty, materials which he uses as he will for the defense and for the victory of Truth. Woe be unto us if we identify our plan with God's, our favorite enterprise with his Kingdom, our dearest possessions with the things that are of final moment in his sight, our party or nation or church or creed with his divine plan.

Into our experience strange and disconcerting things are sure to intrude; if we are anticipating them, we shall not lose the blessing of God's correction and enlargement of our experience. But if we insist upon victory for *our* cause, success for our present plans, the preservation of our dearest possessions and friendships, then we shall not battle as serenely nor as reverently nor as efficiently as did Joab and Abishai. They won their victory that day, for the Syrians and the Ammonites fled before them; but part of the strength and abandon by which they put their enemies to flight was due to the reverence with which they fought, and to the perception of a power mightier than theirs which was not only more precious to them than life but than the victory of their nation.

And as a matter of fact, most noble men are not as fortunate as Joab was. The great loyalties have always accomplished much in the Kingdom of God but rarely what men hoped or even expected to accomplish. The great heroes have drunk the cup of pain with their Lord; they have been baptized with his baptism; but they have not been allowed to sit on the triumphal seats they have envied.

A moment ago we were speaking of John Brown. He risked his all to procure the freedom of the Negroes through inciting them to revolt. His plan was not God's and he failed, but it was in Joab's spirit that he sensed and accepted his failure. Five days before his death he wrote:

"I have passed my time here quite cheerfully, still trusting that neither my life nor my death may prove a total loss. As regards both, however, I am liable to mistake. It affords me some satisfaction to feel conscious of having at least tried to better the condition of those who are always on the under-hill side and am in hopes of being able to meet the consequences without a murmur. I am endeavoring to get ready for another field of action where no defeat befalls the truly brave."

And while his life and his death did not incite the slaves to rebellion and gain their freedom, they did have their place in enthusing the Union forces who in a different way won the victory he seemed to lose.

When Savonarola's body went up in flame on the public square in Florence, no angels intervened as he had expected. He was guilty of a terrible mistake; his plan was not God's nor was his faith the right faith. But that horrible death was, you might say, the back-log of that purifying flame that swept through Europe immediately thereafter. Columbus did not find the short-cut to the East Indies he expected. His plan failed. But his loyalty to the Truth as he supposed it to be was a vital element in the discovery of the Truth as it really was. It is the loyalty of such men to the truth as they saw it that God has built the larger Truth we see.

Why then should we expect our plans to be fulfilled when greater men than we, with their vast loyalties, have had to be corrected by the Almighty? Why are we so overborne when our children turn to careers contrary to what we planned for them, when our financial schemes miscarry, when some great disappointment or bereavement invades our family circle, when some intellectual or moral foundation on which we had builded proves too small or too crumbling for the edifices of our lives? Are we "playing the man" for ourselves and our "isms" primarily, or under all our planning and our struggling and our loving do we still rejoice in the corrective and enlarging presence of God and say, at the beginning and end of every task of ours, "Let us play the man now and always, but let the Lord do that which seemeth him good?"

This then, my friends, is the other basic principle of high manhood, to be convinced that, while we, like Joab, may win our particular battle, especially if we do not overrate the importance of winning it, God is sure to win his. Our courage, whether through defeat or victory, is somehow to contribute to the divine plan which is to be wrought out. It might be a great thing if we could go into every battle sure of winning the victory, but the reality is far greater than that. For we know that if we fight with all our power for the best we conceive, we will help God win a victory greater than any we can see.

Let us then play the man for our ideal, for our loved ones, for our nation, for our church, for our Lord, and let us rejoice not only in the glorious zest of the conflict but also in the serene confidence that our God will do what seemeth him good with us and our fighting and our ideals. Sometimes after the fight is over and defeat has come, God shows us the error and inadequacy of our ideal and gives us a more precious one to defend. And then we are more thankful than ever for the battle-cry in the fight, "Play the man, and the Lord do that which seemeth him good."

ACHSAH'S SPRINGS

And Caleb said, He that smiteth Debir and taketh it, to him will I give Achsah my daughter to wife. And Othniel . . . Caleb's younger brother, took it: and he gave him Achsah his daughter to wife.

And it came to pass, when she came to him, that she moved him to ask of her father a field: and she lighted from off her ass; and Caleb said unto her, What wilt thou? And she said unto him, Give me a blessing: for thou hast given me a south land; give me also springs of water. *And Caleb gave her the upper springs and the nether springs.*

JUDGES 1:12–15

VI Achsah's Springs of Water

A Sermon Preached at Several Women's Colleges

ONE of the surprising things about the Bible, as many of you have discovered, is that while it is an oriental book it portrays the deeds of many women who were in the forefront of public life. Particularly is this true of the primitive times in Israel when the nation, by which God meant to redeem the world, was being fashioned. A surprising amount of space is given to the courtships of Rebekah, Leah and Rachel in the narratives of Genesis. Miriam plays an important part in the Exodus, and in the grim wars which settled the fate of Palestine Deborah and Jael stand out among the few real leaders of that turbulent and impassioned time. Speaking today primarily to young women, it seems quite fitting that I should choose my text from the records of their own sex.

And I speak to you about a woman who some scholars say was originally not a woman at all but a tribe; but, as she is represented to us in the Scripture passage, she is to me one of the most fascinating and one of the most religiously inspiring women in all history. She introduces us at once to an encampment of Israelitish warriors. They are engaged in a life and death struggle. Pushing out from their old narrow home on the border of Egypt, they have spent many years in the desert gathering strength and religious unity. At last they have set out to conquer the "land flowing with milk and honey," the golden apple they have coveted.

The tribe of Caleb has been separated from the rest and finds itself compelled to capture, without guns or battering rams let us remember, two strong walled cities. Against one they have been victorious at great cost and the "giants" whom they fought have yielded to their arms. Hebron is theirs, but Debir still holds out. Some are so wearied that they lack courage for pushing further or even for enduring the constant dread of attack from a watchful and impregnable foe. The leader of the tribe sees probable destruction in following either course, and yet dares not demand too much from his exhausted followers. Appeals to their comfort and to their duty seem alike ineffective. What shall be done? Shall he trust to the general heroics of soldiers and call for volunteers? Somehow a new motive must be found to produce the volunteers.

While he ponders, the figure of his lithesome daughter, Achsah, comes before him—to him and to others a constant source of delight. The motive is discovered. For the honor and the very life of his tribe he will make the sacrifice. Whoever captures Debir shall have not only the city but the captain's daughter to wife!

One man is then suddenly aware of a courage he had not thought that he possessed. The picture of Achsah overcomes the heart of Othniel, himself related to her. Love refreshes the wearied heart of the young chieftain and communicates new courage to his immediate followers. The little band of warriors attacks and carries the stronghold that was too strong for the whole tribe. The grace and beauty of Achsah are stronger than walls and the love of familiar homes. Debir falls to the grace of a woman miles away!

The impetuous victor sends to Hebron for his wife. She comes forthwith riding upon her ass. As soon as we read of her we understand why the love of her gave the victory to Israel that day. She is as clever as she is beautiful and as confident of her power as she is clever. She is a true oriental and does not for a moment dream of refusing the man her father chose for her; she is to be disposed of as he pleases! But while she yields, she means to conquer—and in this she is as much a woman as an oriental!

While on the way to her new lord she has made herself acquainted with the region that is to be her home. She has discovered that Debir is in the midst of a valley which is utterly dependent upon several groups of springs, nearer Hebron than Debir. She talks over the situation with her bridegroom, but the young warrior is too engrossed with his bride to pay much attention to her words. She sees she must act for herself and for her husband—again, not a trait confined to oriental women exclusively. Her mind is made up as to her course. True to that description of a higher love that Paul gives us, she does not behave herself unseemly.

With strict regard for the proprieties of that untutored age, she dismounts from her ass before her father, as did Abigail before David and Rebekah before Isaac. To a woman of power, outward marks of equality are superfluous. She bows with filial reverence to the harsh barbarian who was her father. And then she prefers her request—very modestly and tactfully, but with a sovereignty which precluded any thought of its refusal. "You have set me in the arid land; that is proper, it is your right; I regard it now as my home. You have set me in the arid land; I did not set myself there. Therefore, give me also springs of water."

There is no emphasis on rights; she appeals to his own sense of justice. She does not complain but neither does she cringe. In the height of her beauty and with her father's commanding nature she makes a demand upon her superior. She dismounts, she bends her knee, but when she speaks it is not to curry a favor; it is to remind her father of an unfilfilled duty to her which goes with her prior duty to him. She must dwell in the south, in the arid region, but then he must give her the springs that go with the region. And the rough old chieftain, in order to show his independence of his daughter, refuses to grant her exact request and gives her two groups of springs instead of one!

The charming story which we have chosen for our text, though remote in both time and distance, may bring even to twentieth-century American women a meaningful message. The dignity and the truth in the heart of the barbarian maiden, Achsah, as she approached her barbarian father, give to us something quite real to guide us as civilized Christians in our approach to our spiritual Father, and in the maintenance of a correct attitude before him. I wish therefore to call attention briefly to three important suggestions as to our religious life that this narrative has made to me.

First, we should be as reverent and obedient to the call of our Father in heaven as Achsah was to the call of her father, Caleb. Because we leave out the word "obey" from our marriage services does not mean that we leave it out of our lives. Because we recognize no longer the divine right of kings, it does not follow that we have no sovereign. We can chaff at orientals but we must remember that it is upon their foundations that we have built. The attitude of humility is the only guarantee of progress. The fear of the Lord is the beginning of wisdom.

And this means no vague sort of reverence, no trembling in our closets before we ride on our high horses in the street, but an absolute loyalty to duty, unflinching, quite as a matter of course and with a sense of receiving dignity as we yield thereto. To obey God sounds very grand

and it is sufficiently mysterious for us to incorporate it into our creeds—and do nothing whatever about it. To obey the call of duty is another thing for most of us, a thing about which we feel we have the right to make up our own minds after we have heard the particular kind of call. Which indicates that we are religiously dead and ethically impossible.

To obey God means to obey the call of duty. He does not appear to the most of us in dreams or address us by name, but he does actually hold communication with every one of us in our duty. Caleb showed us in parable what the call of duty is. It was Othniel, who had won a right to Achsah according to the customs of those times, to whom Caleb gave her. It is only somebody or some work that has a right to us that can give us the call of duty. If we turn from the call to duty, we are not religious men and women. Nay, if we hesitate after we recognize it to be our duty, it is not God that we obey so much as our fears of disobedience. The Christian is he that has made up his mind to follow duty even before he discovers where it might lead him.

And we must do it ungrudgingly. It must be a quite natural thing for which we do not stop to praise ourselves. When Achsah mounted her ass for Debir, though it meant a break with all her past, she did not regard herself as a heroine. Part of her life was the obedience to her father. We need not smile at her because she does not step into a limousine. The greatest heroes know little about heroism. The woman whose back was burned to a crisp in the Chicago fire, but whose arms held a living child, was following the deepest instinct of her soul. That is what Achsah did and, let us make no mistake about it, that is what Jesus expects of us: "So likewise thee, when ye have done all, say, We are unprofitable servants; we have done that which is our duty to do."

And we must do it reverently. Whatever high horses we ride when we are among men, we must dismount when we are face to face with duty. We must unsandal our feet before we approach it. "Hallowed be thy name" must have precedence over any petition of our own. When some great duty is presented to us, we are being ushered into the presence of God, into a new era of life. It becomes us to dismiss our gilded vehicles and drop upon our knees.

But—and this is the second suggestion I have mentioned—after we have dismounted, we have the right to prefer our requests. After we have prayed "Hallowed be thy name, thy kingdom come," we have a right to add, "Give us this day our daily bread." And the deeper our reverence and the more unpretentious our obedience, the more natural and the more confident will be our demand for the things essential to the performance of our duty.

When the plans of a life-time are laid aside at the call of duty and an independent woman becomes the nurse of a complaining invalid, she has a right to demand of the God of duty those springs of peace and strength that are necessary for the life of the soul. When one's views of religion are revolutionized, and one is compelled by the deepest needs of the soul to fight the problem through, he has a right to demand of the God of honesty the faith and patience and hope that will keep him from despair. When the closest companion of one's life is taken away, one has a right to demand of the God of death a drink from the spring of immortality. When a man responds to a call to a larger sphere of usefulness in business or profession, he has a right to go to it demanding from the God of his being the strength and wisdom to make the most of it.

In yielding to the call of duty that comes to us we throw the responsibility on God. He has a divine right to send us to any arid place but we have the right of children to the springs that go with the land. If we are summoned to work in the Church we have a right to demand of God that freshness of spirit that shall keep us from the worry that wears men out. Perhaps we have been obedient without being wise. We have lost ourselves in the work or in the prospect of it without making sure of the springs that are essential to the work. We have perhaps dared to take God's vows upon us, as when being received into Church membership, but without trusting him for strength to perform them. We went right from Hebron to Debir without dismounting from our ass and demanding the springs.

God has supreme rights with us, but if he exercises them he must protect those he uses. It is not arrogant to be absolutely confident that God must see us through any task he assigns us. Both individuals and a world in a period of transition have a right to the springs. If at the call of God we forsake old dwelling-places, we have a right to ask him to furnish the new one with necessary springs. If we doubt that he will, we have less faith in our Father than the barbarian maiden had in hers!

That Jesus approves this serene confidence of Achsah in our relations to God is plain: "Seek first," he says, "the Kingdom of God and all these things shall be added unto you." Not a trembling approach to God as though he were a despot, but a trustful demand upon his righteousness for strength to perform his tasks honors him most! As the Epistle of James reminds us: "If any of you lack wisdom, let him ask of God, that giveth to all men liberally, and upbraideth not; and it shall be given them. But let him ask in faith, nothing wavering. For he that wavereth is like a wave of the sea, driven with the wind and tossed. For let not that man think that he shall receive anything of the Lord. A double minded man is unstable in all his ways" (James 1:5–8).

The third and the more indirect suggestion from our ancient story is that God will respond to our call for strength only if we need the strength for our duty. In other words, the springs go with the land. If we go into the arid land, we shall have a right to the springs there, but if we stay at home we shall not. The fact that our Father has springs of water does not entitle us to their possession. We shall get them only if we need them. If Achsah had not been called upon to live in Debir, she would not have asked her father for the springs. She never dreamed of asking Caleb to share his possessions with her simply because they were good things to possess, but only because she needed them.

We must lose the notion that we shall be able to drink from *all* the springs of God. It is only those we need that are open to us. Because accurate scholarship is a spring of God is no reason why we all should expect to possess it; we do not all need it. Because personal magnetism enables one to move others to noble deeds, it does not follow that we shall possess it, for it is perhaps not needed for the duty that God has laid upon us. Because money is necessary in some forms of activity is no reason for us to desire it who really have no need for it. Deep emotion is a spring of power; but that does not mean that we, who work happily without it, need to grumble or to grow anxious if we do not feel the raptures and upheavals of other men. If we would only learn not to weary God and worry ourselves by asking for things we do not need or were not made to receive, how much happier we should be! There are diversities of springs, but there is refreshment in all. Sufficient unto the day is the evil thereof, and sufficient unto the duty is its particular spring.

The path that leads to life for every man is a narrow one. It is no broader than our duty. Let us be content with doing that. No man will exhaust God's springs; let him learn to drink contentedly of those that strengthen him for his own duty, and let others drink from those God has appointed for them. Let us live our own life as individuals, as churches, as denominations, as nations, and drink from our own springs.

Friends, if we learn to obey the call of duty with alacrity and solemnity, if we learn to trust God for what we need to perform it, and if we learn to desire nothing else, we shall understand why the Bible is not degraded by the beautiful barbarian love-story which has guided our thoughts today. No one of us can exhaust all of God's springs, but if we are wise we shall find that our own spring never runs dry. And then we will understand the words of the Gospel: "Whosoever drinketh of the water that I shall give him, shall never thirst, but the water that I shall give him shall become in him a well of water springing up unto eternal life."

GOD'S CHRISTMAS GIFT

Thanks be unto God for his unspeakable gift.

II CORINTHIANS 9:15

VII God's Fourfold Christmas Gift

An Advent Sermon

INDEPENDENCE is certainly a virtue, but only within bounds. We cannot be independent clear through unless we can manufacture the laws of the universe and determine our entrance into the sphere where these manufactured laws of ours operate. And since we cannot do that, a man who makes independence the fundamental virtue we rightly regard as a crank and we leave him gladly in his chosen corner.

It is said that at a big banquet in New York City, after many prominent men had alluded to their homes and their colleges and their employers as sources of their success, a blatant democrat arose. He stuck his thumb in the perpendicular edge of his vest and announced that, for his part, he was a self-made man. He disgusted his hearers as he went on. Then the speaker who followed him began, "The gentleman who has just taken his seat, declaring that all that he is and all that he has done is solely his own doing, has taken a great responsibility off the Creator."

Life is primarily a gift. Men and women are not their own. And the people who recognize that fact, who are not ashamed to be grateful, who realize that the reason they must forgive their debtors is because they can never get out of debt themselves, who feel that no matter how much they give they can never catch up to what they take, who confess that there is a Christmas tree set up in the midst of their lives loaded with gifts—they are the people whom we love. And the day many of them love best is Christmas Day, because on that day the gift they prize the most was made. May I therefore consider with you this morning God's fourfold Christmas gift to mankind?

The first great gift he gave us on the first Christmas Day was Christ himself. So many great treasures have come to us through Christ that we are in danger of letting them smother the fundamental gift of Christ himself. This gift lies behind the forgiveness of our sins, or the Sermon on the Mount, or the parables which have forever enriched the fountains of human speech, or his sufferings on the Cross, or the visions of his resurrection from the dead. It is the character of Christ in itself. What God gave the world on Christmas Day was its supreme personality.

The world had not been devoid of noble men before Jesus lived in it, nor has it been without a great succession of heroic souls ever since. But is there any man, qualified morally and intellectually to judge, who would hesitate to say that in the little hill-town of Nazareth there grew to maturity the supreme figure of human history? As Charles Lamb so notably put it: "If Shakespeare should come into this room, gentlemen, we should all rise; if Jesus Christ should come into this room, we should all kneel."

We can properly say that Jesus is an ultimate word. We cannot anallyze any character without, in a sense, losing it; we cannot take it to pieces and expect to admire the pieces as we admire the whole. But if we are to use our intellects at all with regard to the person of Jesus, we must at least ask ourselves the secret of that manifest supremacy. What is it that makes the character of Jesus the sublimest subject of human meditation? We must search for his power over men not in that which he shared with his contemporaries but in that which he did *not* share with them. They thought that he was "beside himself," so different from them was he. Perhaps the reason why they thought so was the peculiar relationship with God that he arrogated to himself. But the ultimate reason why his own family thought him mad and why some of us might still think him so if he were here, the fundamental reason of his claim to be the Son of God was the fact that he gave love absolute dominion in his own heart and in all his relations to mankind. Hosea and Plato had taken love from the gutter, but it was Jesus who put it on the throne. It has been there ever since.

Now, of course, if a Christian asks "How did he do it?", he can only be answered, "By his living and by his dying." That is where we are driven back again upon Jesus as an ultimate word. That is precisely his secret. Jesus of Nazareth installed a new King over mankind by simply moving before them for little more than a single year. Since then we have been under an altogether new government in the inmost places of our being, where we make all great decisions and experience all transforming emotions largely because a carpenter turned teacher for a few months and walked through a remote province of a dead empire two thousand years ago. That is the most resplendent fact in the history of mankind upon this planet. We crown Jesus Christ King because he crowned Love King. We know now what we worship—not all, but *what*. This, then, is the first abiding gift of God on Christmas Day, the character of a man so miraculous that it has created for us an enduring picture of God.

The second gift is the Bible, particularly the New Testament. Its greatness consists in the demonstration of what the spirit of one man can do for the spirits of other men. The spirit of a man, if you can only get at its highest level, speaks in as universal a language as music. The New Testament is written in what was to Jesus a foreign language. Yet, how his spirit speaks! Turn to almost any page of it and you are uplifted into a world different from ours. The world of the spirit for which we are ordinarily wistful becomes so real that it seems to blot out our own preoccupations. That indeed is one of the dangers; the New Testament seems to tell of so different a country that it is difficult to think of making ours like it, or even of building a strong bridge between it and ours. And yet that is the hall-mark of great literature; it transports you into another world, opens up your spirit by presenting it with vistas not native to it. But this book presents no vistas which were not native to the men who wrote it; they were aroused by another spirit than their own.

The only words preserved for us as they fell precisely from the lips of Jesus are four brief phrases in Aramaic, the native language of Palestinian Jews of the time. They were evidently so peculiarly significant of his spirit that the torrent of Greek civilization could not submerge them.

Abba is the Aramaic word for Father. Both Jesus and the Pharisees seem to have reverently shrunk from pronouncing the proper name of Israel's God, but while the Pharisees usually substituted for it the word "Lord" Jesus substituted the word "Father." They both alike bowed before a great mystery, quite beyond their definition or description, but by this word *Abba* Jesus threw around the mystery the atmosphere of love. And so the Greek Testament preserves this Aramaic word that explains the serenity of the great passages, the stillness of its waters, the green of its pastures.

Talitha Cumi meaning "Maiden, arise," and *Ephratha*, "Be opened," are preserved as the primitive symbols of the holy experience of every soul which opens itself eagerly to the creative forces of this Book, the experience of resurrection and of far horizons. They may be said to express the sovereignty of Jesus, the complete assurance that love is not a weakling but the driving power of the universe.

Eloi, eloi, lama sabbacthani?—"My God, my God, why hast thou forsaken me?"—these words of Jesus as he dangled on the Cross were too precious to sink in a translation. They remain in their nakedness, proudly isolating themselves from all interpretations, as testimony to the cost of the redemption of mankind, and to the utter humanity of its most effectual redeemer.

So do these tremendous Aramaic words of Jesus express the three central qualities of his person, indeed the three supreme attributes of the Christian God—Love, Power, Suffering. Nor can any of us fail totally in experiencing in some degree all of these three.

Through this Book the dullest-eyed among us may catch some suggestion of the love of God, some notion of its miraculous power in animating dead souls and opening undiscovered countries, some sense of the necessity of sacrifice for the perfecting of life. It puts within our grasp the divine elements of human experience. There is no book which is *essential* to the human spirit but this one. It is a glowing record of creative life, picturing ordinary, prosaic, heavy souls made jubilant and powerful by the Master's touch. It is the open, unrestrained witness of the profound delight and satisfaction of men who for the first time had fallen in love with God because they had become convinced that God first loved them. Such a book can never be superseded or duplicated, but it may be read.

God's first gift on the first Christmas Day was a person, his second a book, and the third an institution. If there had been no Christ there would have been no Church. Without the Church, there would have been no *Mayflower*. Without the Church on this continent, there would never have been the sort of liberty which is its supreme glory, nor this particular type of democracy. We may be thankful then for this unspeakable gift.

The trouble with the Church is that, unlike these other complete gifts, it goes on growing, and it doesn't always grow right. It stands for a much bigger thing than it is. It stands for spiritual fellowship, and sometimes succeeds in emphasizing only its lack of it. It has a green garden within it with shade-trees and refreshing fruit, but men often see only what often seems to be a high fence enclosing it. The Book of Revelation is certainly a most inadequate picture of the eternal life, but it ought to be a better description of the Church than it is. Its gates ought never to be shut, except to those who are the lovers and makers of lies. There ought to be four gates open to it from every side of human experience. There ought to be within it a multitude which no man can number who have washed their robes and made them white in sacrificial blood. And there should be choruses of those who sing "Salvation to our God" and who have palms of victory in their hands.

At the heart of every Church, thank God, there *are* such men and women, who can stand the light of the holiest ideal, who know that they are born only to bear witness to the truth, even at great cost. The Church has many faults, among them timidity and bigotry and hardening of the spiritual arteries; but, just as it is, it brings to us a constant spiritual income, because, even though just as it is, it proclaims to millions of us every week a Gospel, a message of Good News that never goes stale: of a God who is not only searching every man but searching for him a triumphant spirit which is bestowed and not earned, of a reward which is too satisfying not to long for, which lies at the heart of sacrifice and robs us of all pride in making it.

God's last Christmas gift is, I think, his best gift. A person, a book, an institution—these are all, so to say, outside of us. His last gift is *inside* of us. It is not a new character to gaze upon, nor a book to read, nor a new institution to join, but a *new heart*. These other gifts we all possess in part by the inescapable fact of living within the stream of life. But perhaps we do not all possess this last one. Yet, if I had said a "new spirit" instead of a "new heart," who among you could say that he is a stranger to it? For Christ is the Saviour of all men, Paul tells us, though especially of those who believe. There is no one of us who has not received some of his spirit and who has not a predisposition for him.

But a new heart is that particular gift of God which comes from a conscious change of control, which is commonly resisted by sinful men like you and me. It may come, I suppose, through the steeling of the individual will to a definite and irrevocable choice; but in that case the gift of God is concealed in the strength of human determination, and the Kingdom of God suffereth violence and the violent try to take it by force. It is certainly far better to pass from death into life that way than not at all.

But the prevailing method of the New Testament is the better way, I think. It is that mysterious experience of feeling the Holy Spirit take possession of the citadel of one's will. It is such a strange and novel experience, and yet so real! It is passing from death into life, for it means just loving God and all his children. Love cannot be commandeered; one must wait for it, or be surprised by it. And when that "possession" comes to a yearning soul, he rejoices paradoxically both in feeling bound by bonds which cannot be loosened and at the same time being set completely free.

This is God's greatest Christmas gift; and I hope that you will not get through this season without a large measure of it. God is love, so it must be coming all the time; don't run away from it. Remember that Christ's truthfulness is staked on this promise: "Ask and it shall be given you; seek and ye shall find. . . . If ye then, being evil, know how to give good gifts unto your children, how much more shall your Father which is in heaven give good things to them that ask him?" This is the gift of the Holy Spirit. This supreme gift is the gift of a loving heart, which must be waited for because it cannot be earned. But to know that that *is* the gift you want, that it is God's to give and that he rejoices in giving it, helps us to wait in hope.

This is a good time to recall the promise made to Israel's king, way back at the dawn of history: "Samuel said unto Saul, The spirit of the Lord will come upon thee and thou . . . shalt be turned into another man. And it was so, that, when he had turned his back to go from Samuel, God gave him another heart." Will God give us less? And if we get that gift, no matter how much we give, we will always be saying, "Thanks be unto God for his unspeakable gift."

A COMMUNION MEDITATION

What will you do unto Jesus, who is called the Christ?

MATTHEW 27:22

VIII A Communion Meditation

THIS question is pertinent for us as well as it was for Pontius Pilate, the Roman procurator of Palestine. Only he did not know how pertinent it was; and you do. So I put it to you afresh today.

Will you ignore Jesus? Ignoring is dangerous business. If done voluntarily, it means the impoverishment of life. You may ignore Washington and Lincoln, if you will, but such ignoring is intellectual expatriation; you are no longer an American—you become a man without a country. You may ignore Galileo, Kant or Darwin, Raphael, Beethoven or Wordsworth, but such ignoring cuts you off from your richest life. You are building your cozy nest on a dead branch, and even birds know better than that. You are deliberately refusing to behold the visions which are making the world new. You are still living on a minor planet instead of in a universe. To ignore them for gay dresses or bank-books or athletics is like measuring a bird's body without listening to its song.

You may perhaps ignore such men as those I have named—and some do, more is the pity—but will you ignore Christ? It seems impossible to ignore him, but there are those who are trying to do it today. There were those who succeeded on the day of the crucifixion. It was not the Pharisees; they left their studies and their synagogues to gloat over his cross. It was not the thieves who were crucified with him on Golgotha's hill; his face threw one into a frenzy and drew the other into Paradise. It was not even the captain of the squad assigned to the execution; he went down from the hanging with the discovery of a righteous man in his heart. It was the riff-raff of the guard who ignored him; they sat with their backs against the cross and diced for his garments. They did not really care to look into that face.

And yet, lower in the scale of brutes than the dregs of the Roman mercenaries is the man who today is careless of Christ. Impulses that have made nineteen centuries noble have had their rise in him. To ignore Christ today is to cut yourself loose from the inspiration and driving force of the Christian world. If you do so, the petition that you are offering to the God who answers prayer is actually this: "O God, take thy Holy Spirit from me."

Or will you patronize him? That is what Pilate did. It is much more respectable than to ignore him. Judges, tycoons, leaders of society sometimes do that, rather than the riff-raff of a Roman soldiery. The very preposition in the question hints of patronage, "What shall I do *unto* Jesus?" I suppose that Pilate thought that it did not matter greatly what he did. He fancied that the fate of Jesus was in his hands, because it was granted him to prescribe the time and method in which the soul of Christ was to slough off its body. But Pilate had very little to do even with that. The soul of Jesus did not depend upon an unjust crucifixion of his body for his Lordship over mankind. Almighty God never gave Pilate leave to decide the spiritual destiny of man, whatever Pilate might have thought.

But Pilate's patronage of Jesus was not only official; it was also moral. He had examined his prisoner and he was really very well satisfied with him. He found in him no fault at all. Of course, he had no idea of *living* so obscure and pitiful and wandering a life; but he had concluded that it was really a very good life in its curious way, quite harmless and blameless.

Jesus answered Pilate never a word. He does not allow a man to take liberties with him. Yet there is a great host of men as respectable as Pilate who are doing just that today. It was Pilate, not his prisoner, who stood before the judgment seat. And now, after Jesus has unified and ennobled the leading races of mankind, when he has for most of us the value of God, the attitude of patronage toward him reveals, in the creature who assumes it, nothing but an abysmal vulgarity. To be a patron of the arts, in this sense, is crude enough; to be a patron of Jesus Christ is insupportable.

Yet that is really the attitude of a man who finds, with Pilate, no fault in him, who approves his life in the main, but who has no slightest thought of living it himself. He protects Jesus from the criticisms of others through his gracious admiration, but inwardly admits that it is too poor and lowly a life for him to live. He looks down upon him from the loftier heights of modern civilization, from the more respectable pursuit of money, from the cultured leisure of a well-appointed study, or even from the halls of justice where Pilate sat before him. Yes, they say, he is a good man; a splendid thing for the poor and the suffering; and then the patron smiles with a touch of self-congratulation, pays his pew-rent, and is off.

Off from more than he knows—from the aspirations of the best, from the mighty deeps of the soul, from a glad carelessness of what the world regards as success, from the peace of God. This is the despicable attitude I fear for some of us. Let no man see any of us poor sinners extending our gracious patronage to the Son of God. He does not need our admiration.

But what *will* you do unto Jesus, who is called Christ? The chief priests and elders all say, "Let him be crucified." And that answer was much more suitable than the answer of the rude soldiers or of respectable Pilate. The leaders of the Jews had not behind them a religious ancestry for nought. They knew spiritual power when they saw it, and they saw it in Christ. When such a spirit was in the world, they could not any longer be at ease with phylactery and Torah. They saw that he was dangerous, that if his spirit continued its fascination their authority and their ideals, even their nation, were all shattered. He was a man that must be reckoned with, must be put out of the way.

And he must be put out of the way disgracefully. His spirit was strong enough to survive anything like an exile or an ordinary death. The enthusiasm of his followers could be checked only by legal disgrace and public shame. He had blasphemed, hadn't he? He had promised to give freely, and without their consent, that peace which their fathers had taught them to expect as a reward of perfect obedience to the Law, hadn't he? Their patient waiting for God out of the heavens was only a prelude to lording it over the whole world, they believed.

And here was one who was living a life that struck across all of their dearest ambitions. He did not care for lording, and he said that God did not either. Before the peace and wonder of his life they grew alarmed. All their fasting and tithing seemed to have been for a goal that this man rendered cheap, even to them. The people were leaving them, for in this man they apparently found what they wanted. These official leaders themselves began to become superfluous, and I have no doubt that they inwardly began to grow suspicious of their own life-purposes and the divinity of their own ideals. If they were to be able to be comfortably selfish again, they must crucify this Jesus. He was far too great a figure not to declare war to the death upon.

And, my friends, if you are inalienably in love with yourself, you must do the same thing. If you serve God for what you think you will get out of it, you are obliged to declare war on Jesus. Or, if you are not serving God at all, and are here for a short span of years only for luxury or pleasure, then you must declare war on him.

The Pharisees, the religious egotists, and the Sadducees, who believed in neither angel nor devil but only in gold and position, were hereditary foes; but they struck hands to nail Jesus on the cross. The chief unhappiness in your selfish life is the same as theirs. It is the presence of Jesus in your world. One or the other has to give way, either your love of self or Jesus Christ. "I am not come," he said, "to send peace but a sword." Where that peerless leader approaches, swords must be taken from their scabbards. Shall they be drawn for or against him? There must be a crucifixion: shall it be of yourself, or of your King?

When you return home, you that despise the ruffians of the guard and the patronage of Pilate, ask yourselves which you can live best without, yourself or Christ? Make plain what it means to draw your sword against Jesus, the friend of publicans and sinners, the Jesus who "spake as never man spake." Erect your cross and decide which you will drag to its foot, yourself or your only possible guide to the life of God.

The question, therefore, presses for its answer: "What shall I do unto Jesus, who is called Christ?" And as the disciples were eating, Jesus took bread, and he gave it to them and said, "Take, eat, this is my body." What shall I do? What else is there to do save to take and eat? What is there for any honest, yearning man to do save to identify his life with Christ's as he takes and eats? To give to him our wills and to beseech him for his spirit?

GOOD FRIDAY

Walk worthily of the Lord.

COLOSSIANS 1:10

IX A Good Friday Sermon

THIS command of the apostle never seems so much out of place as on Good Friday. To walk worthily of Jesus Christ seems at all times beyond our power, but today surely it seems presumptuous. How can we walk worthily of him who for our sakes hung upon the Cross in inconceivable agony?

Moreover, are we not inclined, as normal human beings, to shrink from this dark day of human history, and from cross-bearing as essential to an ideal life? If to walk worthily of the Lord means to do the things he did in the spirit in which he did them, do we wish to walk worthily of him? And we cannot forget those unequivocal words of his: "He that doth not take his cross and follow after me is not worthy of me." Good Friday is a recurring judgment-day. Not to *wish* to walk worthily of him is another thing, and an inexcusable thing. Yet, should we celebrate Good Friday by evading the test of Good Friday?

We recur therefore to our text, "Walk worthily of the Lord." It is a command that has to do primarily with our purpose, not with our accomplishment. And yet we cannot long cherish a purpose which we conceive to be impossible. After we have once heard the high demand, we cannot forget it. Does not Good Friday itself keep us from renouncing discipleship? We must *wish* to work worthily of him. Is there any wish that is higher or deeper in a Christian heart? Is there anything we wish more than to be disabused of the idea that it is an impossibility? I wish today to advance three thoughts which seem to me to make it less impossible to work worthily of him and which seem therefore to make it less necessary to write *Failure* over the face of our Christian life at the start.

In the first place, Jesus Christ would never have offered the great sacrifice of Calvary for those unworthy of it. He would have degraded himself to the ranks of the sentimentalists or of the sensationalists if he had permitted himself to offer up an unworthy and unnecessary sacrifice. He did not deem it so. "He knew what was in man" and, because he knew, he felt himself justified in dying for man in the fearful torture of the Cross. Our worth is not to be measured by what we do, but by what is done for us by the just and the clear-sighted. When Jesus laid down his life deliberately for our salvation, he may be justified only if our salvation be worth his sacrifice. He believed it was; else he would not have made it. We believe it was, because we believe in him. And when we are forced to the belief that we are worthy of his death, we have become holy in our sight.

We know Jesus well enough to be convinced that he would not have been moved to this deed on Calvary by the *numbers* to be saved. If a thousand souls are worth saving, one is. We are absolutely sure that Jesus would have borne that same pain if it were only our souls alone—my soul alone—that he would thereby have redeemed. And so we have become holy to ourselves, not because of anything we have done or anything that we have seen in ourselves, but because of what Jesus has seen in us and because of what Jesus did for us.

It is by this subtle path of the spirit, it is through the revolutionizing of our estimate of self, that the merits of Jesus Christ have rendered us holy. To him and to God we were holy before the sacrifice was made, to ourselves only afterwards. It is our forgiveness by *ourselves* that Calvary made possible, notwithstanding all the sins with which we disgust ourselves every day. We will bear with them longer, we will refuse to give ourselves up as impossible, we will regard ourselves as holy—because Christ died for us.

And with far deeper meaning than the poor lover of Maud, we perforce say:

> But if I be dear to someone else,
> Then I should be myself more dear.
> Shall I not take care of all that I think,
> Yea, ev'n of wretched meat and drink,
> If I be dear,
> If I be dear to someone else?

We *are* worthy of the Lord, then, my friends. Not if we seek to make ourselves so, but because he gave himself *for* us. And this is a great help to us in walking worthily of him. It robs the highest purpose in the world of presumption.

The second thought is this: To shrink from the Cross is not unworthy of Christ; it is like him. He gave thanks indeed as he went to the Cross and with sublime faith. He offered himself as the lamb for God's supreme burnt offering with sublime resignation. His sweat was, as it were, drops of blood, so did his agony in the Garden lay hold of his vital forces. And his prayer was, "If it be possible, remove this cup from me." It is no unreal man who is our Master. He healed sickness. He took little children in his arms. He had nicknames for his disciples. And he shrank from his Cross—Gethsemane is the hard victory of a man over his full desire to live, not the final spasm of a fanatic.

To shudder before we lay ourselves on the operating table, to shrink with terror from the repeated knocking of an incurable disease on the door of our plans and hopes, to prefer joy to pain or life to death, to hesitate before renouncing a favorite ambition or a harmful intimacy or a cherished questionable business advantage, is not to be unfaithful to Christ. And if we once realize that to follow Jesus Christ does not mean an inhuman and supposedly angelic delight in suffering, I feel that we shall not find it quite so impossible to walk worthily of the Lord.

And the third thought is this: Jesus does not ask us to bear his cross but our own. "He that doth not take *his* cross and follow after me is not worthy of me." Jesus came to his Cross in the way of his duty. The only cross we are called upon to carry comes along the way of our duty.

This does not banish the cross from life. We are not trying to erase Good Friday from its lofty position. The way of duty does not skirt Golgotha; rather it goes to it and through it, for us as for Jesus. As Mr. Lowrie has said in his beautiful study of the Lord's Prayer: "The swimmer is not aware of the current unless it runs counter to his course. To feel God's will in its sharp distinction from ours is to know it as duty. The great symbol of duty is the Cross."

And yet there is so profound a majesty at the heart of duty, we are so miraculously strengthened and elevated at her approach, that to bear a cross upheld by her, and enlarged and transfused by her, is not impossible. It is, even for *us*, almost inevitable.

For in Gethsemane, Jesus was choosing not between life and death but between two kinds of death, certainly between two kinds of sacrifice. He had to give something up. He had to part either with the favor of God or with life. He had to choose either the Cross or the betrayal of his own soul. And he saw that dear as his will was to him, the will of God was dearer. The Cross was the way of life not only for the world but for himself. Terrible as was the fearful anguish of the midday torture on the Cross, it was not so terrible as to live without God. Had Jesus foregone the Cross, he would have been his own Judas. He chose fearful torment, but he rejected worse.

And there is no more divine manifestation of the priceless worth of duty, and of the joy over which she alone disposes, than the kiss with which Jesus met Judas and the steadfast glory with which he set his way to the Cross. He saved our souls because it was his duty to save them; he saved our souls by saving his first. The greatest sacrifice in human history, its holiest altar, does not condemn the world by cheapening all our sacrifices, by dwarfing all our ideals, by exhibiting a heroism which is utterly beyond our comprehension and which removes Jesus from the imitation and companionship of human kind.

The Cross of Christ is like ours; his sacrifice was made possible by his duty, made inevitable by it. His duty was unique, just as his soul was unique and his lifeblood a unique ransom for many. But his duty reveals the sublimity, not the triviality, of ours. He came into the world not to condemn the world by the unapproachableness of his perfection, but to save the world by the actual unfalteringness of his spirit. The words of First Peter are not fantastic words: "Christ also suffered for us, leaving us an example that we should follow his steps." We *may* follow, after all. We may not suffer on his Cross, but we may suffer on ours. We cannot do his duty, but, following him, we may do ours.

And it seems to me that we shall walk worthily of our Lord if we bear our cross in the spirit in which he bore his—bear it not because we do not shrink from it or because we do not feel it, but because it has become inevitable by becoming our duty.

In the light of this thought, we ordinary disciples of Jesus may understand the familiar words of Paul which may have seemed unreal before: "Let your manner of life be worthy of the gospel of Christ, because to you it hath been granted, in the behalf of Christ, not only to believe on him but also to suffer in his behalf."

The apostle evidently means that it is a boon to suffer in behalf of Christ. And is it not, after all? For if we are driven to choose between Christ and wealth, or between Christ and lust, or between Christ and the Church, or even between Christ and our parents, and really discover that we choose Christ, it means suffering, of course, but it reveals the fact that we know that for us Christ has become inevitable. When we choose our cross and undergo our deprivation and stretch ourself out to a lifelong conflict with fleshliness or ease or friends, letting ourselves be nailed to it by our love of Christian duty, we are indeed crucified with Christ.

"Without shedding of blood," says the writer of *Hebrews*, "there is no remission." Unless our devotion to duty and to men and to Christ is sufficiently deep to cause us agony, to give us the zest of choosing Christ and duty instead of something less, our service will have in it but little of healing or of power. But we need not seek crosses. We *must* not seek them. Only when they loom before us let us give thanks that we have come to that point in the Christian life when the contrast between the world and Christ has become clear to us and when the love of Christ outweighs for us, as it surely will, the allurements of the world.

May we not go then from this place to walk worthily of the Lord through the power and compulsion of his own grace, which is sufficient also for us?

ON IMMORTAL LIFE

Who knoweth the spirit of man whether it goeth upward?

ECCLESIASTES 3:11

He hath set eternity in their heart.

ECCLESIASTES 3:21

X Meditations on Immortal Life

An Easter Sermon

IN these two sentences from the relentlessly sincere Book of Ecclesiastes, we have the two apparently unchanging truths which underlie all our meditations on immortal life. The first is the ever recurring question, "Who knoweth?" The second is the unquestioned fact, "He hath set eternity in their heart." It is well indeed to have the most sacred day of our religious calendar set aside for a consideration of this momentous theme. Let us consider it today as sincerely, as humbly, as reverently as we can.

At first sight the question above seems to land us in the darkness of materialism. But does it? Think of the facts which a materialist would see. Man after man comes to his death like a beast. After his death he is buried. His flesh decays, falls asunder, is lost, like a beast's. The bones never come together, we believe, as in Ezekiel's vision. Million after million, men are gathered thus to the dust; the same end happens to the righteous and to the wicked alike. In dreams by night men have seen them, much more rarely in visions by day; but the dreams have passed, the visions faded, and the bodies always turn to dust. Why not accept these facts, consider the matter settled, eat and drink seeing that tomorrow we die. Why question any more?

Why? Because the questioner is *not* a materialist. He is a man who is looking around, who is examining, who has not yet come to a conclusion. And he is a questioner because in his heart, as in ours, God hath set eternity. If he were merely a materialist, the undoubted fact of the universal and irrevocable dissolution of the body would settle the case. But being an honest questioner, he sees something more.

"The spirit of man," he asks, "who knoweth whether it goeth upward?" When he rolls up the stone to close the sepulchre, he is not sure what he is shutting in. There remains in him the hope of immortality.

It is set in his heart. As sincere and honest men, we may take our stand with him. Immortality can be for every man of us at least a glorious perhaps. The closing of the grave does not close the question. One of the most infallible signs of a humble and enlarging spirit in a man is the ability to keep that question open. As eternity has been set in our heart, it is our privilege to keep it there. It is not a thought of our own devising. It is at the very heart of our noblest living. I can do no better than to suggest ways in which it has been set there.

First of all, God has set eternity in our hearts by giving us the desire of immortality. In this we are not peculiar. So far as our investigations can carry us, men almost universally have refused to regard death as the end of life. The mind of man cannot accept the idea of total extinction. The hope of immortality is a *prejudice* of human life, and it is a difficult prejudice for a living man to eradicate. It can be done only by a deliberate setting of the will, and its effect is the impoverishment of human energy. It is setting one's nature against one's nature and is therefore bound to fail. Animals may become extinct without diminishing their energy while alive, but it is only so because the idea of their own death has never occurred to them. To postulate one's own extinction is to paralyze one's power of living. The very instinct of life forces us to keep the question of immortality open.

But eternity has been set in our heart also by our noblest intellectual tradition. When human instinct counters human tradition, as it often does, there rises a momentous spiritual conflict. But when they coincide, there seem to be revealed to us the fundamental elements of our existence.

Why are Plato's dialogues of *Phaedo* and *Phaedrus* immortal? Certainly not because of the intellectual arguments by which they seek to establish the immortality of the soul; such contentions are interesting chiefly to the historian. These works are immortal because they set the highest human ideas in the light of immortality and disclose the glorious fact that only in that light do they become clear and full of power. Take Plato's great words, *beauty, courage, self-control, justice, wisdom,* or take the great words of Christianity, *faith, love, peace, forgiveness, sacrifice,* and see how they "come alive" in the light of immortality.

Take, as a single illustration, the word which spans so many centuries of human thought, the word *duty*. How little duty recks of compensation of the world! How ill she takes protests based on common utility and visible results! With what imperious tones she calls us to what often seem trivial tasks! From what alluring pleasures she holds us back to learn some facts and dates of history soon forgotten, to add up some stupid figures, to write our letters home, to take our sleep and exercise! How little we seem to accomplish at her dictates and for what small results she invokes eternal values! No matter! Even at the death bed some of us have found her standing. At that moment there is nothing ahead to influence; our last hour may at least be free of her. But she refuses to treat it as the last hour; she looks death squarely in the face, turns from it, and commands us just as usual.

She apparently regards all the circumstances and tasks of life as parents do the sandpiles they provide for their little children. In her eyes, they are simply means by which she is preparing us for joys and duty in a sphere beyond our sight. Duty elbows off the sneers and doubts of the superficial strata of our being and pushes us, in our own despite, into an eternal realm. And who is there of us who does not yield to her, who does not acknowledge her right to her imperious tones? Who is there indeed who knows

> " . . . anything so fair
> As is the smile upon her face?"

We all of us live in our highest moments on her assumption that we are immortal spirits. And, thank God, most of us know that we see more truly in our highest moments and that

> "Tasks in hours of insight willed
> May be in hours of gloom fulfilled."

As Goethe said long since, "If we do not believe in another world, we are dead for this." What man before me does not agree with the words Tennyson wrote in the second *Locksley Hall*, after the death of his son Lionel?

> "Gone for ever! Ever? no—for since our dying
> race began,
> Ever, ever, and for ever was the leading light of
> man.

Truth for truth, and good for good! The good,
the true, the pure, the just—
Take the charm 'For ever' from them, and they
crumble into dust."

This is Easter. On this day God has set eternity in our hearts most convincingly as we turn to the most brilliant pages of human history. Nothing is more certain in the records of the race than the inspiring and invigorating and purifying influence of Christianity in the beginning of its mighty career. And nothing is more certain about the power of Christianity than its dependence upon its assurance of immortality.

We read the letters of Paul and John today with respect for their intellectual ability but chiefly with abiding gratitude for the exuberance of their joy in immortality. That joy clarifies their judgment, exalts their motives, tinges nearly their every page with glory. We still read them as letters from home. They bring us glorious tidings of the immortal realm, and, as we read, we discover that it has never been far from any one of us and that in it we "live and move and have our being." The impression they make upon us is the impression which the apostles and their converts made upon the ancient pagan world: "Jesus and the Resurrection" was the message which transformed the world.

And that double message was really one; neither came to its own without the other. I cannot explain the appearances of Jesus after he had expired on the cross. I do not know whether or not the tomb was empty, whether or not it was thought to be empty even at first. I do not know how the apostles differentiated between those marvelous visions of the risen Lord from other similar visions which were no stranger to them. The only thing that is certain is that they believed them, that they were changed by them in the core of their being, and that they witnessed to that conviction in such a manner that they were undeterred by death, and that they convinced of the life everlasting men who despised both their religion and their intellect and their race.

If we are to judge a faith by its effects, a tree by its fruits, then the visions of Easter Day are the most important facts in the whole of human history. Those visions and a firm faith in them united a multitude of races into a single family, even such opposites as proud citizens of Rome and Pharisee-fanatics of Judea. And the family characteristic was earthly sacrifice steeped in heavenly joy. Sometimes the joy was too intense to express rationally, but it was too real and too elemental not to spread. Diverse in character, in tradition, in ideals and in culture, all these converts were basically alike. They had been baptized into the same spirit, which was all aglow with eternity. Whosoever received that spirit was released from earth; their joy was of a different sort from any round about. The spirit which came upon them, without merit or without expectation of their own, was the spirit of an endless life.

But men will not always be satisfied with judging a tree by its fruits. They demand also the opportunity of judging it by its roots. Why was it that these men saw such visions? Why were they proof against the skepticism of the scintillating Graeco-Roman culture? Who was it that these men saw in the robes of immortality? Could he wear them without presumption and blasphemy?

So the whole world gathered about the Man of Nazareth. And what by common consent have they found? A man in whom is found the complete assurance of immortality! He was as certain of the coming of the Kingdom of God as were the Romans of the coming of a new Caesar. Heaven was to him the most secure place possible for the storing of treasure; it was earth that was in his eyes uncertain. He knew that he was of kingly rank, but with him the insignia of royalty were humility and service. "Jesus," we read, "knowing that the Father had given all things into his hand and that he came from God and went to God, took a towel and girded himself and washed the disciples' feet." Reverent acts of service were his favorite material for constructing the bridge from this passing world of sense to the abiding world of the spirit.

It was from the realm of immortality that he drew, with undeviating sureness of selection, the elements of the one sublime character mankind knows. Not only did this man, before whom all the world still kneels in amazed reverence, believe in immortality, but that belief was at the very core of his being; without it he could not have been. He wrought with human hands the creed of creeds, and one of its very few articles is, "I believe in the life everlasting." So implicit in his every act was that belief that he could discover the spirit of immortality where no one else had been able to find it.

One day the Sadducees confronted him with a question that was designed to uncover the embarrassment of everlasting life. They believed that God never would add to the Law of Moses and that he could not have omitted to tell Moses that life was eternal if it were really true. After answering the question, Jesus added, "But as touching the dead, that they are raised, have ye never read in the very Book of Moses, how God spake unto him, saying, I am the God of Abraham and the God of Isaac and the God of Jacob?" Why, of course, they had often read those words, but what did that have to do with the resurrection of the dead? To that unspoken question he replied, "God is not the God of the dead but of the living."

It was as clear to him as the day that whomever God once loved was loved forever. The love of God could not descend upon a man without immortalizing him. The man whom God loves is as certain of living as God is. Neither will outlive the other. God of Abraham, God of Isaac, God of Jacob belong together. If indeed love is the divinest reality in the world, then immortality is the surest. Jesus' disciples saw only after his death what he had seen all through his life.

Thus the man of Nazareth made the visions good. The immortal life was lived on earth before men saw that it was bound to outlive the earth and in another and mysterious sphere. As John begins his letter on Immortal Love, "That which was from the beginning, which we beheld ... and our hands handled ... we have seen and bear witness ... unto you that eternal life which was with the Father was uncovered unto us." Jesus and his resurrection confirm and illumine each other.

The hope of immortality, then, dwells in virtually every breast because love does. Into the mystery of love we cannot enter today. But we can at least say of it that it is the power which transforms human character and human vision through the reverent perception of human virtue. Love and courage and self-sacrifice and peace are not self-existent ideas; great as they are, they are qualities of something greater even than they. They are elements of the human soul. If they are immortal, the human soul must be.

Perhaps nothing is more instructive on this point than the oration which Robert Ingersoll delivered over the grave of his brother. His faith in God was weak and, so far as we know, his affection for his brother was not exceptionally strong. But as he stood by that grave and thought of the struggle and the character and the goodness of the man whose body he was consigning to the grave, the hope of immortal life burst from his lips: "Who knoweth the spirit of man whether it goeth upward?" Even the thoroughly agnostic Ingersoll could not close the question and accept as final the evidence of the destroyed senses. He seemed to feel that there was something holier, more authoritative than the senses.

And out of this same experience with human character, as we see it and revere it in men and women, spring deathless poems of our own times and language. Out of it rise, for example, Matthew Arnold's *Rugby Chapel* and *Immortality*, Browning's *Prospice* and *Epilogue to Asolando* and *A Grammarian's Funeral* and *The Ring and the Book;* out of it, and above all, Tennyson's *In Memoriam.* William James' analytic but chiefly reportorial work, *Varieties of Religious Experience,* glows with a faith in immortality. As we read such works and meditate upon the experience out of which they spring, one thing becomes quite certain for us. It may not be a conviction of immortality, but it is a conviction that the holiest and deepest experience of human life takes it for granted.

> "Oh me! What profits it to put
> An idle case? If death were seen
> At first as Death, Love had not been . . ."

The hope for immortality, then, is the high and common hope of the race. So deeply has God set eternity in the heart of man that, though we trust our senses day by day and do not find ourselves deceived by them as guides for action, we refuse to trust them in the presence of death. Instead, we then trust the spirit that the senses only serve, the heart of man in which God hath set eternity so deep that it cannot be uprooted. It inheres in life itself; it is reinforced by our holiest and widest and most persistent traditions; it is confirmed by the most glorious pages of human history. It is at the heart of the highest of the sons of men. It enters into the experience of the humblest when we are at our best. It insures our self-respect. In the midst of agony, of disappointment, of obscurity and loneliness, it fills us with amazed gratitude to God, our Friend.

We cannot prove immortality; we must leave the question open. But if we do this, we must live as though it were true. For the hope of immortality cheapens mere earthly aims; it is too deeply set in our hearts not to mould our souls. For that hope and by that hope we must live. And so, though we may not prove immortality, we shall be living the immortal life.

MEMORIAL DAY

Forasmuch as ye know that ye were *not* redeemed *with corruptible things, as silver and gold, from your vain conversation received by tradition from your fathers; but* with *the* precious blood *of Christ, as of a lamb without blemish and without spot.*

I PETER 1:18–19

XI Calvary in the Light of Memorial Day

THERE is no easier approach to the heart of a man than to make demands upon his loyalties, which really measure his spiritual stature. Whatever the unforgivable sin before God may be, we feel sure that before men the unforgivable sin is disloyalty. We have an unconscious longing for objects, causes, persons who can command our loyalty. When we set our faces toward college, for example, we expect an education but we expect even more an object of devotion. The man who has made most of his college course is the one who carries away with him for life two great loyalties, the loyalty to his college and the loyalty to the Truth. The worth of a man is indeed disclosed quite accurately by the quality of his loyalties.

Tomorrow will be Decoration Day. While this holiday has now largely become a time for recreation, no one of us forgets the sacrifice which it commemorates. Once more men, old and younger, will parade in uniform and place little flags on carefully selected graves. And I wish to treat this Memorial Day as an approach to Calvary, for I feel that the profound truth of our text stands out more vividly with the help of Gettysburg and Antietam, of Chateau Thierry and San Mihiel, than with the help of the theologies of Anselm or Grotius. As we earnestly search our memory, the holiday becomes indeed a holy day.

The startling statement, "Ye were redeemed with precious blood," loses all sense of unreality as we think of the men who gave themselves to establish and preserve our country in times of national crisis. Most nations are builded as Hiel built Jericho: he laid the foundation of it with the blood of his first-born and set up its gates with the blood of his last-born. America, at any rate, was founded with the blood spilled in the War of Independence, and its gates were set up for all men with the blood of the Civil War. We enlarged those gates with blood in the war with Spain. We insisted that they remain open in World War and we confirmed that purpose with blood.

This country, like all the great countries, is a product not merely of inescapable evolution but of completely voluntary sacrifice. It owes its power not only to those who have enriched their lives by living for its ideals, but to those who have forfeited their lives by dying for its ideals. The prosperity and freedom that we enjoy today are sanctified as we realize what they have cost. Each Memorial Day reminds us anew that the country which protects our lives and offers us so many diverse opportunities of service is not a thing which was flung gaily off from the wheel of the Creator in a trice, but something so holy and sacred that God incited men to lay down their lives for it. Their sacrifice creates a holy obligation which exalts every man who feels it.

Mankind has cherished for three thousand years a story of the semi-barbarian David, second king of Israel. Carried by the fortunes of war near the gates of his home-town, he called out thoughtlessly in the heat and discomfort of battle, "Oh, that one would give me water to drink from the well of Bethlehem!" Three soldiers heard, broke through the lines of the Philistine enemy and brought the water to their idolized leader. "But he would not drink," says the ancient record; "he poured it out before the Lord." What men give their lives for belongs to no man; it is God's. And David said, "Shall I drink the blood of men that went in jeopardy of their lives?" It certainly is no more honorable for us than for David to appropriate men's blood to selfish ends.

To regard this country for which men have died as merely a convenient place where we may build our houses, erect our colleges, exploit our talents and hoard our earnings, is to repudiate a sacred obligation and to empty our life of much of its sacred meaning. We have accepted the security and liberty of this country as the basis of our individual lives. Unless we remember that they are the price of blood, we are devoid of the finer sense of honor. Memorial Day makes service to our country a thing of duty. We have been paid for it already in blood. Every American that lives today has been redeemed from the terror and ignominy of a foreign domination by precious blood.

In the light of this fact, may I ask your reverent attention for a few moments to the place of the death of Jesus in the Christian life? Memorial Day convinces us without much argument that blood *does* purchase things that money never can, and it shows us that the atonement of Jesus is not something abnormal or irrational, but of the very warp and woof of human life. If the blood of ordinary men purchased a country for us, it is to be presumed that the blood of Christ purchased something more, and then indeed our loyalty to him is not to be likely to be overdone.

What then has the blood of Jesus Christ purchased for us? He did not die for his country; he died *by* his country. He died for something higher; it might almost be said that he died precisely because he believed that there was something higher. Like the heroes of our great wars, he was permitted to die for a great cause. Like them he was permitted to establish his cause by his death. Their blood has purchased for us the consciousness of a free and united country; his blood purchased for us the consciousness of a loving God.

"A man is worth," said William James, "just as much as that about which he busies himself." The great men of the world are as deathless as the causes with which they had the power to identify themselves. The reason for the supreme place of Jesus Christ among men is that he identified himself with God. Other men stand for liberty, for patriotism, for science, for reason. This man stands for God.

God and he had the same purposes and aims; but not so other men. But he did not on that account love men less; superficially considered, it would seem as if he loved them more. He lived with God, but he died for men. It was the lost sheep that he went to seek; it was the lost boy upon whom his heart dwelt. There was nothing on earth that Jesus found more sacred than the love in his heart for wayward men; there was nothing in the sacrifices of the Temple, nothing in the holy commands of the ancient Law, to compare with it. Therefore he knew that God loved men as he loved them. He ate and drank with publicans and sinners not because he wanted to make a sensation, nor because he wished to see how the other half lived, but because he loved them and because God loved them. He had no feeling of condescension in fraternizing with those whom God loved.

Jesus believed, moreover, that the most powerful force on earth was this love of God for which he stood, which he shared and which he carried. He believed that men could be saved and that they were to be saved most easily by love. The Pharisees who stood for the Law failed, and the priests who stood for ritual. He seemed to believe that love had a better chance.

And no man ever loved so widely, so unsparingly of self, with such high hope, with so pure a heart. The love he carried was not mere human affection; it was divine love. He did not long for men's devotion but for their joy. From men he asked nothing but the privilege of serving them. Hence history knows no such blend of courage and humility, of wrath and tenderness, of self-esteem and self-sacrifice. He alone knew —no other man had tried it—that the life of love bound a man to God and his fellows but freed him from himself. And so he was compelled to assert that the cure for sin was love, that the cure of self was love, and that love needed no cure.

And it was for this that Jesus died. Men would not have it so. They wished to criticize; he wished to inspire. They wished to judge; he wished to forgive. They wished to rule; he wished to serve. They wished to get; he wished to give. And they killed him because of their hate of his ideal. And he has brought us, and the people of over fifty generations, to his God by his precious blood. Because he was lifted up, he has drawn all men unto him.

Had he flinched, we would have regarded him as one impostor more. Had he drawn back from the Cross, the love he proclaimed with such spotless purity and such constraining force would have perhaps found little hearing and would have lacked the final proof. Other men have suffered as much as he, but no man has bought so much for men by his suffering as he. His identification of himself with God was revealed when he died for God's children simply because they were God's. The Cross bought for men the consciousness of God.

None of us, therefore, can ever accept from his lips and his life the blessing of the boundless love of God without remembering the price that was paid for it. In the midst of all our joy and pride in our country, Memorial Day comes to us saying, "Remember what freedom cost!" In the midst of all our trust and joy in God, in the midst of the glad service of men this trust begets, the Cross of Christ appears as though saying, "This is what your spiritual freedom cost!"

In all lands and in countless deeds of reverent service, Christ is seeing of the travail of his soul, but it is the travail of his soul that has produced them all. There is no denying the fact that ours was the life won, and his the life laid down. "With his stripes we are healed." And therefore we have the right to sanctify our lives with the supreme loyalty to Jesus

Christ. We have not run merrily along our way into the loving arms of a heavenly Father. We are not our own. We have been bought with a price. We have been redeemed with precious blood.

Surely there can be no sense of outrage or of unreality as we listen to the solemn words of Paul: "Are ye ignorant that all we who were baptized into Christ Jesus were baptized into his death? For the love of Christ constraineth us, because we thus judge that one died for all, therefore all died; and he died for all, that they that live should not longer live unto themselves but unto him who for their sakes died." That certainly is the logic of every honorable and grateful Christian.

Thus then is our right established to the great underlying loyalty of our life. The Cross of Jesus Christ is not to be regarded as an easy escape from the penalty of sin; it is not to be regarded merely as the supreme manifestation of the love of Christ—though it is that; but it is to be regarded as the price of our delight in God and man, and therefore as the measure of our own devotion. What Jesus bought with his blood we stand ever ready to defend with ours.

Years ago a young girl killed General Minu, the tyrant of Moscow. She had never heard of Nathan Hale, the hero of our Revolutionary days, but in words almost like his she said—I think she said it at her trial: "Wherever I may chance to die, in prison, on the gallows, in the mines of Siberia, I shall die with but one thought—Forgive me, my people, that I can give you so little, only *my life*." Can we not make some such prayer to our Lord?

THE HOLY SPIRIT

And it came to pass, that, while Apollos was at Corinth, Paul having passed through the upper coasts came to Ephesus; and finding certain disciples, he said unto them, Have ye received the Holy Spirit since ye believed? And they said unto him, We have not so much as heard whether there be any Holy Spirit. And he said unto them, Unto what then were ye baptized? And they said, Unto John's baptism.

Then said Paul, John verily baptized with the baptism of repentance, saying unto the people, that they should believe on him, which should come after him, that is, on Christ Jesus. When they heard this, they were baptized in the name of the Lord Jesus. And when Paul had laid his hands upon them, the Holy Spirit came on them; and they spake with tongues, and prophesied. And all the men were about twelve.

ACTS 19:1–7

XII The Descent of the Holy Spirit

MANY people, my friends, fail to recognize the difference between *believing* and *receiving* the Holy Spirit. Paul went about on his mission, endured his hardships, performed his mighty works and wrote his timely epistles, not because he believed something but because the Holy Spirit had come upon him. Indeed, the object of all his preaching and working was not to induce a belief but to impart the Spirit.

Here in Ephesus he found a group of twelve men who had believed but were without the Holy Spirit. Exactly how they came by their belief it is impossible to discover. They had been baptized but they had not thereby received the Holy Spirit. Paul apparently concluded that they had been baptized only into the name of John, and that they had gone no further in the religious life than the Baptist; for, no matter what they had believed or through what religious rite they had gone, they had not received the one distinguishing mark of the early Christian fellowship, the peculiar experience which made all who had enjoyed it members one of another. They had not received the Holy Spirit; nay, they had not even heard that there *was* a Holy Spirit.

The Apostle Paul, all aglow with a power that enabled him to accomplish what before had been impossible, treated the twelve as heathen and insisted upon a genuine baptism in order that they might receive the genuine Christian experience. To Paul at least, the mark of a Christian was not a new creed but a new heart, not a new belief but a new character. We have not yet—not all of us—discovered that peace and power are not determined by articles of doctrine, by the number of things that a man is prepared to assert about God and man, but by the quality of the inner force which drives him on. Some of us are strangely like those twelve men; we are often so content with intellectualized religion that we have not even heard that there is a Holy Spirit. Like the devils we believe, but unlike the devils we do not even tremble.

From its inception, Christianity has not been a new belief but a new Spirit. Jesus did not teach a new creed; let us not forget that he simply accepted the Jewish creed, for it is quite impossible to distinguish the intellectual basis of the Old and the New Testaments, otherwise we would not make of them a single volume and call them The Bible. He did not even teach any new commandments. He replaced the ten commandments by two commandments, it is true, but he did not compose those two—he simply quoted them from the Scripture of his people. What then was the new element which came into the world through Jesus of Nazareth, so unmistakably new that Jesus himself said that new vessels would have to be found to contain it?

The Gospels themselves are in no doubt about it. The oldest among them, the Gospel of Mark, begins thus: "The beginning of the gospel of Jesus Christ, the Son of God. . . . And John . . . preached, saying, There cometh one mightier than I after me, the latchet of whose shoes I am not worthy to stoop down and unloose. I have indeed baptized you with water: but he shall baptize you with the Holy Ghost.

"And it came to pass in those days, that Jesus came from Nazareth of Galilee, and was baptized of John in Jordan. And straightway coming up out of the water, he saw the heavens opened, and the Spirit, like a dove, descending upon him: and there came a voice from heaven, saying, Thou art my beloved Son, in whom I am well pleased" (Mark 1: 1–11).

The new element in Christianity was a new Spirit; it was to Jesus as though it had come from heaven for the first time and made its initial home in his heart. It was because of it that Jesus recognized himself as the Saviour of mankind.

This the Church has not always remembered. We often find ourselves declaring that the condition of salvation is belief on him, and that the holiest task is to imitate him. But we find him declaring that there is something holier than he is, something far more important for men to understand than any mystery of his person, for the condition of salvation is not salvation itself.

He heard men one day murmuring about him. He had just been restoring health to the mentally diseased. And men of strict righteousness and blameless life, who were quite unable to do as he had done and who therefore recognized in him quite a different spirit from their own, were saying to one another that his spirit was an "unclean spirit." And he turned and said to them: "All their sins shall be forgiven unto the sons of men and their blasphemies wherewithsoever they shall blaspheme; whosoever shall speak a word against the Son of Man, it shall be forgiven him; but whosoever shall speak against the Holy Spirit, it shall not be forgiven him, neither in this world or in that which is to come."

It was this Holy Spirit that gave to him all his significance for men. Because of that reality he wrote no creed, he insisted on no ordinances, he set up no school, he established no organizations, he announced no program. He spent his brief public life transforming men by his spirit. Therefore it was that we find him quoted in the fourth Gospel as saying, "Except a man be born again, he cannot see the kingdom of God; except a man be born of the spirit, he cannot enter into the kingdom of God." He seems on one immortal occasion even to regard his own personal presence as an obstacle to the redemption he was bringing, for he is reported as saying by one who understood him as few have ever done, "It is expedient for you that I go away, for if I go not away the Spirit will not come into you." It is what a man lives by, not what a man lives beside of, that determines his quality, his power, his destiny.

Similarly we find his greatest apostle specifically declaring, "Whosoever hath not the Spirit of Christ is none of his." In view of this cumulative testimony from all parts of the New Testament, should we not let Paul ask each one of us, as well as those twelve men he found in Ephesus, "Did ye receive the Holy Spirit when ye believed?"

The answer of the disciples of Ephesus was, "We have not so much as heard whether there be any Holy Spirit." I hope that that answer would not be justfied in the churches of our time. And yet that answer makes me somewhat uncomfortable. I fear that some of us ministers are so anxious about the welfare of the Church or so taken up with establishing the preeminence of the character of Christ, so enamored of his beauty and so given over to adoring it, that we are in great danger of forgetting the very heart of the Gospel, namely, the one absolute essential of the Christian life—to have dwelling in our hearts the very Spirit of God, to be baptized with that self-same holy baptism with which our Lord was baptized, and to know that there is a Holy Spirit and that its natural dwelling place is in our hearts.

Now, my friends, I quite recognize that we ministers are not altogether without excuse for this deplorable condition of spiritual affairs. The doctrine of the Holy Spirit has been in the past so sternly and so fantastically preached that many of you laymen, so far from upbraiding us for our silence on the very heart of our religion, have been inclined even to outdo these Ephesian disciples and say to us, "We do not so much as *wish* to hear that there is a Holy Spirit. The tongues and prophecy which followed on its reception by these Ephesians do not attract us. We are quite content with our recognition of Jesus as rightful leader and with our rather lame, but not altogether abandoned, efforts at keeping the commandments." But are we? Are we happy about the prevailing spiritual lassitude among us? To be honest with ourselves, don't we wish to be "born again," to know at first hand the raptures of regarding our bodies as temples of the Holy Spirit?

Yes, we do shrink from the Holy Spirit. But this shrinking comes, my friends, from a total misapprehension of the Holy Spirit. It is not some uncontrollable, convulsive and unaccountable force which throws men and women into ecstasy and leaves them after a few days or weeks in misery and exhaustion. It is a mighty Spirit, it is true; it does control and never allows itself to be controlled; it transforms without asking permission; it almost invariably induces moments of transport. But none of these statements about it describes it—each one simply calls attention to some one of its effects or its outer characteristics.

A few moments ago I said that Jesus laid down no new commandments, but simply reaffirmed two old ones. But we read that he said, "A new commandment give I unto you, that ye love one another." This puzzles us, for we find as far back as the Book of Leviticus the words which Jesus explicitly quoted from it, "Thou shalt love thy neighbor as thyself." Why does John make Jesus call this a *new* commandment? We read further, "A new commandment give I unto you, that ye love one another; even as I have loved you, that ye also love one another. By this shall all men know that ye are my disciples, if ye have love one toward another."

Yes, that's it! The new Spirit that came into the world through Jesus was the Spirit of his own peculiar love—that love which sprang into being because Jesus opened his heart fearlessly to the love of God and which developed its joy and power by pouring itself as something consciously divine, and upon every human soul whom it touched. The new element in Christianity is not the *command* to love but the *power* to love, the Spirit of love shed abroad in men's hearts, the inevitable necessity of loving because the heart is so full of the surprising and unmerited love of God. And when we hear from Jesus that God is more willing to give the Holy Spirit to them that ask him than parents are to give good things to their children, it means that God is eager to give to every man who will have it the power to love him with all the heart and mind and strength, and every neighbor as himself.

Do you want that Spirit? If so, what you have to do is nothing else but to open your heart to the love of God and expect to receive it. If you want not merely to understand but to possess the Holy Spirit, think this moment lovingly of all men. Let your first act on leaving this place be an act of love for love's sake. Let yourself go. For Jesus came into the world for no other reason than that every man should, in looking at him, long for the Spirit of love which glorified his life, and then should open his heart to receive it. And when it comes, really comes, so that all selfish ambitions seem tawdry and every opportunity of kindness is recognized as a gracious visit of Almighty God to your soul, then will you know why Paul treated the men without the Holy Spirit as heathen, then you will know the peace that passeth understanding.

May I read to you an extract from the letter of a man who, after having discovered on a trip to the Holy Land this secret of the Lord and apprehended its simplicity and bliss, thus wrote to a friend of his?

"Take my day's actions. I arose at eight; I looked out of the window; I noted the line of cabs and cabmen in front of the hotel; then and there came the choice of looking at them sympathetically or unsympathetically. I could dwell upon their harsh voices and rough ways, drawing back from them in my will, or I could reflect that they were seeking employment anxiously in order to support the wife and children whom they love.

"Unconscious of me, they joked and brushed their cab-cushions, but up at the window I was choosing the world of good-will or of ill-will as my momentary dwelling. The same choice I made as I sat at the breakfast-table and was attended by the waiter; in my slight conversation with him came the opportunity for the significant choice of good-will rather than ill-will, resentment or tact and friendliness. When I noticed that he had forgotten the hot water for my coffee, I did not draw back in my spirit, but I reminded him gently and I thanked him when he corrected his omission.

"Thus throughout my day which is nearly gone I could name twenty, yes forty, points where the orbit of my conduct has intersected the orbit of other human beings, and each time I have had an opportunity, great or small, important or trivial, to express kindliness or to surround myself with an aura of chilling reserve; but, such as they are, these simple experiences make up the sum of my life and essentially of all our lives."

I have chosen this particular illustration of the working of the Holy Spirit to set alongside of Jesus' casting out of evil spirits, in order to make it perfectly clear that it is a temper of the soul rather than any particular result of this temper. The author of the letter you have heard was converted to this spirit while on foreign travel, hence the peculiar experiences that came to him. The opportunities and contacts would of course be different and might be harder in the home or office or school, but the spirit of eager love for men and gratitude for being permitted to manifest it would be the same. That Spirit is the holiest thing in the world, the supreme reality which makes the world holy.

We read in the text that this transforming Spirit came upon these dreary believers in Ephesus when Paul laid his hands upon them. Some peculiarly organized minds have thought that it came to pass because Paul was an Apostle, but the real reason was because it was Paul himself. It is so today. The Spirit of God is transmitted by the contagion of a loving personality. The Church of God throughout the ages has maintained a succession of such spirits, and that is its supreme function. They are not hard to find; they ought not to be hard to become. For the chiefest delight of the Christian is to have his heart filled with love and to let it overflow upon his friends and neighbors—and his enemies. And remember always that it is God's supreme delight to bestow it upon men who will receive it.

WASHINGTON & LINCOLN

And when the messengers of John were departed, he began to speak unto the people concerning John, What went you out into the wilderness for to see? A reed shaken with the wind? . . . A man clothed in soft raiment? A prophet? . . . Yea, I say unto you, and much more than a prophet. This is he, of whom it is written, Behold, I send my messenger before thy face, which shall prepare thy way before thee. . . . Among those that are born of women there is not a greater prophet than John the Baptist; but he that is least in the kingdom of God is greater than he. And all the people that heard him, and the publicans, justified God, being baptized with the baptism of John. But the Pharisees and lawyers rejected the counsel of God against themselves, being not baptized of him.

And the Lord said, Whereunto then shall I liken the men of this generation? . . . They are like children sitting in the market place, and calling one to another, and saying, We have piped unto you, and ye have not danced; we have mourned to you, and ye have not wept. For John the Baptist came neither eating bread nor drinking wine; and ye say, He hath a devil. The Son of man is coming eating and drinking; and ye say, Behold a gluttonous man, and a winebibber, a friend of publicans and sinners! But wisdom is justified of all her children.

LUKE 7:24–35

XIII Washington and Lincoln

A Sermon for Patriot's Day

THIS dramatic passage in the Gospel of Luke is full of authoritative suggestions from Jesus our Lord on some of the deeper problems of life, but today, for lack of time, we must neglect most of them. The episode does provide, however, an admirable background for our consideration, on such a day as this, of the richness of our American heritage in possessing, as our two most revered national heroes, men of such contrasted types as Washington, the father of our country, and Lincoln, its preserver.

The two great religious leaders among the Jews in the presageful first century of our era were John of the desert and Jesus of the town. Two figures could hardly have been more different, and at the same time more devoted to the high service of God. Jesus was not vague in his manner of thinking, and his good will toward men did not obscure in his mind the vital contradiction between John's attitude to life and his own. He does not seek to gloss it over in order to relieve the multitude before him from its perplexity. He tells it plainly—he always told everything plainly—that there was a great difference between John and him.

John held himself aloof from the common pleasures and habits of life; Jesus entered into them heartily. John was an ascetic like most of the leaders of religious life in the early ages of the Church; he came neither eating bread nor drinking wine. Jesus took the things of earth as he found them; he did not emphasize the negatives; he came eating and drinking. He and John lived totally different lives and possessed divergent ideas of the will of God. And, according to our record, Jesus told all this to the people. But he told them something besides. He told them that both John and he had the same source of inspiration, but he hinted in his ever-present humility that neither John nor he exhausted that source, and left them with this wonderful sentence of our text to direct them to a unity larger than any they had dreamed about; "Wisdom is justified of all her children," he said. "Both John and I advance her holy cause."

Just as wisdom in a single generation was served by John of the desert and Jesus of Nazareth, so in the same century America was served by Washington the aristocrat and Lincoln the plebeian.

Washington came from royalist stock. His ancestors left England because they were harshly used by the Puritans. His father was a prosperous Virginian, owning broad acres, mines and ships. On the death of his brother, who had married into the English nobility, he inherited the estates of Mount Vernon and took a first place in the aristocratic society in which he moved. A well-dowered bride made him the richest man in his colony. As he had already been the most judicious and one of the most popular, his prominence in the affairs of the colony was inevitable. He was a natural financier, mastering the details of a varied business with celerity and acumen. He served in the House of Burgesses, was chosen to command the colony's troops in the French wars, was sent as one of its five representatives to the Congress in Philadelphia and made such an impression there that John Adams, in remote Massachusetts, declared him immediately, by virtue of "his skill as an officer, *his independent fortune*, his great talents and his excellent universal character," to be the one man who would command the approbation of all America as the General of the colonial army.

He was chosen as a representative of the wealth and standing of his colony. His friends were of old and honored stock. His servants wore carefully chosen livery imported from England. His bride rode in a coach; and he bought a new one for himself just before he went to the Congress which made it impossible for him to ride in any at all for a long period of years. He made trips to Philadelphia for balls and horse-races and theatres. He conformed without much sense of conformity to the social habits of his time. His own individuality uttered itself in the traditional civilization of the day.

He believed not only in the old Church year and in the old celebration thereof, but also in the old distinctions of position. He believed in authority and delighted in exercising it. He rode on horseback all the way to Boston from Mount Vernon to establish the precise nature of his command in the campaign against the French. For the sake of inspiring terror for authority he hung mutineers instead of shooting them. When Commander-in-Chief he burst out on Alexander Hamilton, whom he loved beyond all other men, with, "Sir, you have kept me waiting at the head of this stair for ten minutes." On his presidential trip to Boston, he compelled the sick and reluctant governor of Massachusetts to be carried to him on blankets to make the call he imperiously demanded. As Woodrow Wilson said of him, "He exacted the uttermost farthing." He was a masterful man as aristocrats are wont to be.

When we turn to our other patron saint, what a different man looms large before us! How ungainly the frame, how ill-fitting the clothes! An early friend called him "the ungodliest figure he ever saw." It is doubtful if he ever wore so expensive or fashionable a suit as Washington's coachman. He rode to his first term in the Illinois legislature in borrowed raiment; he had none of his own fit for such splendor.

Though of good sturdy Anglo-Saxon stock, it had become much down at the heels when he entered the world out of it. His father was a wanderer. His mother was of low origin and owed her reputation for her high jumping in mountain revivals. Abraham climbed to his bed on a loft by pegs driven in the wall, doubtless glad that the bed was not laid on the dirt floor. He was an unsatisfactory farm-laborer, a failure as the proprietor of a country store, where he lost more money than he ever had possessed. His law-partner tells us that it is doubtful if he ever read a law-book through and reports many a case he lost by sheer ignorance of elementary legal detail. He was impatient of all precedents, fond of quoting Calhoun's dictum, "to legislate upon precedent is but to make the error of yesterday the law of today." He always tried, as he expressed it, to get his case "clear of technicality and swung to the jury."

He had no genius for taking pains, much for avoiding them. He was slovenly in his personal habits, and vulgar and obscene in his language if thereby he could preserve a joke. He was a born independent as Washington was a born conformist. Hence he threw over the religion of his companions and found his hard way to his own, and only after much of his life was spent.

There is an odd similarity in some aspects of their outward careers. Each was a good surveyor early in life; each was a captain in an Indian war; each a President and a Commander-in-Chief. But how differently they behaved in their similar stations!

While Washington was a loyal Episcopalian—vestryman I think—Lincoln was a free-thinker. While Washington indulged in the convivial habits of his time, though with considerable restraint, Lincoln refused to touch either alcohol or tobacco because he could see no sense in either. Washington hung Virginians for incipient mutiny and set his face like a flint to teach New Englanders reverence for authority. Lincoln was himself condemned to carry a wooden sword for a flagrant breach of discipline. When Washington was made a captain of a single regiment instead of a colonel of several, he resigned his captaincy in dudgeon. After the regiment which Lincoln commanded in the Black Hawk war was mustered out, he gladly enlisted as private in another.

Of his honor and his right Lincoln was as careless as Washington was tenacious. Instead of making a sick governor of Massachusetts visit him, Lincoln threw all custom to the winds and went himself to pay visits he had a right to expect his generals to pay him. "I would hold McClellan's horse if he would bring us victory," he replied to a protesting friend. He sat at his cabinet table inquiring and weighing opinion, instead of directing it. "Did Stanton call me a fool; I guess I must be one." His sympathies were all with the lowly, even with the outcasts. In his first inaugural, he gloried in the fact that, though many an officer had deserted the Union for the Confederacy, not a single private had proven unfaithful to the Union flag.

Washington sought to dominate the people; in the middle of his second term as President, father of his country though he was, men spoke widely of impeachment, of treason, of misappropriation of public moneys, even of assassination. Lincoln sought to learn the people's own will, confident of their essential rectitude, knowing himself but one of them. Though he died by a bullet, it took a madman to fire it. He was a grave and reverent man, reverent before men as well as before their God, as a democrat is sure to be.

The men were very different, the Virginia aristocrat and the backwoods lawyer from Illinois, yet their cause and their devotion were the same, and they stood with the same humility before God and duty.

Their cause was the same; they both were inspired by a love of a sacred ideal to which they gave the same name, liberty. It was liberty which dwarfed the ease and opulence of Washington and it was liberty that robbed Lincoln of his daily fear that he might take his own useless life.

It was not a war of aggression which they waged, these two Americans; it was a war of the defense of sacred rights. It was for liberty they fought —they called it so, both of them—though they did not mean quite the same thing by it. Washington fought for the rights of inherited opportunity, Lincoln for the inalienable rights of manhood, but they both fought for freedom for a man to grow in.

Washington proves that an American may be an aristocrat. Yet there is a type of aristocracy that is almost treason in America—to hold, namely, that a select group of men is better than another group. That was not Washington's type. "He was," as President Wilson has said, "an aristocrat by taste, not by principle." He sought special company, but he sought for that company no special privileges.

And Lincoln proves that an American may be a democrat. Yet there is a certain type of democracy that is almost treason in America—to hold, namely, that all men are equal and then to *denounce* those that prefer other society to yours and that outstrip you in an open field. And that was not Lincoln's type of democracy. As poor as any man in this house, almost as poor indeed as Jesus of Nazareth, he neither coveted nor denounced riches. He loved a man for his manhood. In his eyes, riches could neither spoil nor enhance it. And so this aristocrat and this democrat fought under the same banner of freedom and loved it equally.

They loved it *equally*, I say. And neither of them held anything back. At the outset of the war Washington said simply to his neighbors: "It is my full intention to devote my life and fortune to the cause we are engaged in, if needful." And at the close of it, when he heard that his nephew who was in charge of his estate had regaled with refreshments the English who were threatening Mt. Vernon, he wrote him: "It would have been a less painful circumstance to me to have heard that, in consequence of your non-compliance with their request, they had burnt my house and laid my plantation in ruin."

And Lincoln was as ready to sacrifice his prospects as Washington to sacrifice his possessions. He deliberately lessened his chance of defeating Douglas for the Illinois senatorship that he might maneuver him into a position where he would be forced to shatter the party of slavery as the price of victory. At his own defeat he calmly said, "Though I now sink out of sight and shall be forgotten, I believe I have made some marks which will tell for the cause of liberty after I am gone." After his first term as President, for example, instead of seeking to succeed himself, he attempted to bestow the Republican nomination on Horatio Seymour, Democratic governor of New York, in order to weaken the forces of the opposition.

And Washington and Lincoln served liberty, not only with the same devotion, but with the same humility. Their great powers, measured by their cause, were insufficient. It was in humble reliance on the God who made the cause so vast, who made it indeed holy and impregnable, that they put on and took off their armor. As Washington resigned his commission at Annapolis, he said: "My gratitude for the interposition of Providence . . . increases with every view of the momentous contest . . . I consider it my indispensable duty to close this last solemn act of my official life by commending the interests of our dearest country to the protection of Almighty God and those who have the superintendance of them to His holy keeping."

And Lincoln, in leaving his townsmen for the Capitol, before some of whom he had spoken foolishly of religion, said to them: "I now leave, not knowing when or whether ever I may return, with a task before me greater than that which rested upon Washington. Without the assistance of that divine Being that ever attended him, I cannot succeed. With that assistance I cannot fail. Trusting in Him, who can go with me and remain with you and be everywhere for good, let us confidently hope that all will be well."

So, my friends, if these noble and diverse protagonists of ours are in a peculiar sense manifestations of the American spirit, then to be an American means not to share those qualities and attributes which differentiated these men from each other, but to possess the spirit which invigorated them both alike. It does not mean to be rich or to be poor, to be either of an historic or of an obscure family, to be either aristocratic or democratic in our personal tastes, to be dictatorial or tactful in our methods. To be an American means to possess that which Lincoln and Washington had in common, an undying love of liberty and a complete devotion to its unending furtherance, a sure sense that the cause of freedom is the cause of God. Indeed, America and liberty are so synonymous to me that I believe Carl Schurz was precisely right when, shut out of Germany in 1848 and sailing for America, he said, "Ubi libertas, ibi patria."

I wish that the holy cause of liberty were today triumphant in the world. But that is not the case, and on this day we have the duty to enlist under its banner for a conflict as tense and as far-reaching as those in which Washington and Lincoln led. They, like Jesus and John, are indeed proof of the eternal truth of our text, "Wisdom is justified of all her children."

Yes, the conflict has been joined, for the crusade for liberty is eternal. The only way in which it may be met by Christian men is clearly indicated by the great plebeian himself: "It is for us to be dedicated here to the unfinished work which they who fought at Gettysburg so nobly advanced. It is for us to be here dedicated to the great task remaining before us, that we here highly resolve that these dead shall not have died in vain; that this nation, under God, shall have a new birth of freedom; and that government of the people, by the people, for the people, shall not perish from the earth."

IDEALS & INSTITUTIONS

Woe unto you, scribes and Pharisees, hypocrites! for ye pay tithe of mint and anise and cummin, and have omitted the weightiest matters of the law; judgment, mercy and faith. These ought ye to have done, and not to have left the other undone.

MATTHEW 23:23

XIV The Conflict between Ideals and Institutions

IN these words Jesus indicated his solution of one of the most pressing and inescapable problems of every thoughtful human being—the relation between man's ideals and the basic institutions of society. Roughly speaking, ideals stand for the future and the institutions for the past and every man owes allegiance to both.

The ideal calls man to tasks unaccomplished; to "an adventure brave and new"; to the promise that he has seen and greeted from afar and that has made him aware that he is but a stranger and a pilgrim upon the earth. It gains much of its peculiar sanctity from the fact that it has never been realized and that he sees that it must be; it gives value to his soul; it discloses to him that he does most for his fellow-men when he refuses to imitate them, when he "presses on toward the mark of his high calling." By its newness, its unaccomplishedness, its call to complete a great, imperfect structure, it lays hold on his soul. It makes him appreciate the words of Mary Lyon: "I have asked God to keep me alive just so long as I can do something for Him which no one else can do."

The institutions call man to a reverence for the past out of which his soul, with its cargo of ideals, has sailed forth. They call him to both humility and gratitude. They remind him of the inexorableness of time. They bid him treasure his three score years and ten by the immutable strength of their foundations. They declare that we all are "like grass which groweth up: in the morning it flourisheth and groweth up; in the evening it is cut down and withereth; whereas in their sight . . . a thousand years . . . are but yesterday when it is past and as a watch in the night." All the ages have been building upon them; all the ages have been cradled in them; all the ages have fled to them at the approach of their austere ally, death. Our lives have drawn their richest sustenance from the gardens which their walls surround. It is from them that we have gained the leisure and the inspiration to form these ideals which now dominate our souls.

And for every normal man much of the confusion of his life consists in being commanded by these sacred institutions to be loyal to the past and being compelled by his ideals to be loyal to the future. The most sacred forces known to mankind draw us simultaneously forward and back.

And this conflict of ideals and institutions is not only the struggle of past and future to obtain possession of a man's soul. It is, again to speak roughly, the conflict between his social and individual personality. We are made up, in large part, of relationships with each other and of what Jesus would have called our relationship with God. Institutions are the organizations which guard the second commandment, "Thou shalt love thy neighbor as thyself." They keep order and proportion on earth. They create society out of chaos. They enable us to begin centuries ahead of our ancestors. They guard us against bestiality and bestial individuals. They make sure that the noblest attainments of the past are not despoiled by the instincts of barbarism. They satisfy that large part of us that is not our own, that part of us that belongs to society, that could not exist except within it.

But that is not all of us. There is a part of us that can never be organized or institutionalized.

> All the world's coarse thumb
> And finger failed to plumb
> And passed in making up the main account,
> All instincts immature,
> All purposes unsure
> That weighed not as his work, yet swelled the man's amount.
>
> Thoughts hardly to be packed
> Into a narrow act,
> Fancies that broke through language and escaped,
> All I could never be,
> All were ignored in me,
> This I was worth to God whose wheel the pitcher shaped.

And this private part of us, these divine aspirations of ours, this bent of our souls for which all the machinery of civilization seems to have been installed, all this bows in sacred reverence not before society but before God. It glories in the *first* commandment, "Thou shalt love the Lord thy God." And it knows that it is the fruit—a fruit irrevocably bound to the second, but the fruit after all. It is through this personal individual part of us that we come into closest, most unquestionable, most immediate communion with God. And we know that we shall make a bad bargain if for the sake of that which we owe to the sacred institutions of society we sacrifice that ideal of our own by which we lay hold of the Divine.

This conflict is vital and immediate to us all. No one who has taught in college or church can well ignore it. The teacher or preacher has his supreme opportunity presented him by the university or the church, yet he is not primarily their servant. He has taken the opportunity presented by them because he would fain bring his listeners under the spell of a holy, unrealized ideal. Yet, without the university or the church we should not have come within earshot of the heavenly voices which resound within their walls and which transport us to another sphere.

It is fortunate therefore for us that Jesus incorporated this conflict, in which we are all caught, in a life which has arrested the attention of the world and should have taught his disciples, in the words of our text, their own attitude toward it.

To begin with—perhaps, in a sense to end with—it is perfectly clear that Jesus did not regard his soul as enmeshed in society. When he spoke these immortal words, "What shall it profit a man if he gain the whole world and lose his own soul," he ranged himself with the individualists. A man can lose everything except one thing—his own soul. That he dare not lose. And he dare not lose that, not because of its value to society, but because of God and eternity.

The circumstances of his time and the convictions of his soul were such, moreover, that he waged war for the ideal *against* the institution. The Church and the State were bitter enemies in Judea. But in order to do away with Jesus, Church and State joined hands. Not only did Herod and Pilate become friends, but the Pharisees and Pilate became co-laborers. It took all the combined forces of Church and State to erect the Cross on Calvary. And the Family and School did nothing to prevent it. The Family may have wept, as though over a son they thought of as deranged. The School had virtually outlawed this teacher as a disturber of the peace. All the great institutions of society were either actively or passively engaged against him. The Cross was erected by earth's most sacred institutions. But, since Jesus hung upon it, it has been regarded forever as earth's holiest ideal.

Jesus of Nazareth shrank from that Cross, as all men with ideals to propagate shrink from death, but he never dreamed of asking Church or State or Family to save him from it. He asked God but God said No. So the great choice was before him—the choice between the institutions which stood for holiness and order and human affection and human wisdom on the one side, and his own single soul's discovery of truth on the other. And so quick and uncompromising was the choice that we hardly think of it as ever having been made. He died for us all, but that is only a sublime figure of speech. He died first of all for his own soul—for his ideal.

Certainly there can be no doubt as to which side Jesus ranges himself in the high conflict which we are considering. The future, rather than the past, is his. The ideal is more to him than all institutions; the human soul is of more value to him than any sacred time-tested organizations—nor can any of us claim to be his disciples if we transfer our ultimate loyalty from the ideal even to the basic institutions of our society. It is then no wonder that Church and State denied him and accomplished his suppression.

What is wonderful is that Jesus should have supported at all the institutions which suspected or outlawed or murdered him. And yet there is no more doubt of the fact that Jesus was loyal to the fundamental institutions of humanity than of the fact that his supreme loyalty was reserved for the ideal. Our text is a magnanimous edict of tolerance for institutions by the supreme idealist of the race. Nor does it stand alone in the Gospels, for he was often called upon to render a decision on this very conflict between the institution and the ideal. It is most interesting to observe that he met it and answered it specifically in relation to each one of the four great institutions of society.

Our text answers it for the Church. It is taken from the virulent denunciation which he poured out upon the strongly-entrenched churchmen of his time. "Woe unto you," it scorches, "Scribes and Pharisees, hypocrites! for ye tithe mint and anise and cummin and have left undone the weightier matters of the law, judgment and mercy and faith, but these ye ought to have done *and not to have left the other undone.*"

Most idealists now would have ended that sentence differently. They would be inclined to say, "These ought ye to have done *rather than* the other." But not so Jesus. He approved of tithing, even to the smallest possession, to mint and anise and cummin—spices and weeds. One tenth of all to the great institution! Only judgment and mercy and faith, over which no institution can dispose, must be cared for. There is a place for the Church if only that place is recognized as distinctly subordinate to judgment and mercy and faith.

In the preceding chapter in Matthew, the same issue is brought to Jesus to decide between the ideal and the institutional, only this time it is with reference to the State. All monarchists—and indeed all patriots—are right in underscoring the answer of Jesus, provided they underscore it all.

"Master," said the Herodians, "we know thou teachest the way of God in truth and regardest not the person of men." They recognized him as an idealist. "Tell us, therefore, what thinkest thou? Is it lawful to give tribute to Caesar or not?" "Show me the tribute money," he replies, and they do so. "Whose is the image?" They say, "Caesar's." Then he saith unto them, "Render to Caesar the things that are Caesar's and to God the things that are God's."

It was as if he had said, "Now bring me a soul. Whose image is stamped on it?" And Jesus answered once for all, "Pennies to Caesar and the heart to God." Caesar has his place; the pennies declare that. But when you compare Caesar's place with God's place, you are weighing a penny against a soul. Do not think that you can manage without a State or without a Church. Maintain them both loyally, but as those whose springs of action are subject to neither.

At another time Jesus met the same conflict between the ideal and the institution in connection with education. It was of course in connection with religious education, for then the sciences were unknown and history was profane. But the principle is the same, whether the college be fundamentally ecclesiastical or fundamentally secular. In this case we do not know the exact details of the issue; but the alleged pronouncement of Jesus still surprises all radicals by the excess of its conservatism.

"Then spake Jesus to the multitude and to his disciples," so Matthew begins. "The Scribes and the Pharisees sit on Moses' seat: all things therefore whatsoever they bid you, do and observe; but do not ye after their works, for they say and do not." Now I confess that if this verse stood alone, I should be inclined to think that here the institutional is permitted for once to smother the ideal. As long as teaching comes from authoritative instructors it must be followed. If you have no better men to put on Moses' seat than the Pharisees, then you must do as they say. But it looks as if Jesus really thought that so long as the teachers spoke for Moses, they could not wander far enough from the truth to justify revolt from their teachings. It was only when they set out for themselves that they were to be disobeyed.

But we cannot help remembering the Sermon on the Mount, with the saying, "It hath been said by them of old time," quoting the books of Moses, and with the sovereign, "But I say unto you." These utterances of Jesus do not seem to be in harmony and so I must leave them discordant. But, however you may be able to reconcile them, they at least suggest the presence in Jesus of both the radical and the conservative, and the assurance that the highest personal vision of the individual need not displace his loyalty to the institution which maintained that great body of truth from which his own individual vision had sprung. There was no doubt in Jesus' mind that he was greater than Moses, but neither do we have any doubt but that he and Moses were in the same spiritual movement.

Much the same temper characterizes Jesus' attitude toward the bitterest and tenderest of all conflicts between the ideal and the institutional, when a man is compelled to choose between loyalty to his ideal and loyalty to his home. How greatly Jesus revered the family is shown both by his teaching and his life. To keep out the ravages of lust in the fearfully fleshy days in which he lived, he condemned the Mosaic freedom of divorce. To keep out the degeneracy of avarice he attacked the provision of the scribes which made it lawful for a man to pay his temple-tax in lieu of supporting his parents. For thirty years he was gladly subject to his own father and mother.

But when the crisis came he acted as an idealist must. When his mother and brethren, deeming him "beside himself," came to the house where he was teaching and asked him to come to them, he set himself far from the sacred ties of family affection and, looking around upon his disciples, said, "Behold my mother and my brethren. For whosoever doeth the will of God, the same is my mother and sister and brother." And who can forget that terrible saying, "Whosoever loveth father and mother more than me is not worthy of me." The ideal has precedence over Family, as over Church or State or School; and even to one who loves them all.

It seems to me then that the attitude of Jesus in this fundamental question is clear. We may agree or differ with it, but we cannot misunderstand it. It is the attitude of both the true conservative and the sane radical. It is perhaps the most difficult of all attitudes to maintain spiritually. It is to give the supreme loyalty to our own ideal at whatever cost, to count all things—all historic institutions as well as all personal possessions and associations—as loss in comparison with that which brings us and God in instant and constant contact, and confers worth on every action of ours and on every inner aspiration. But it is also to understand so thoroughly and so gratefully how our own ideal has sprung out of the loins of the past that it becomes a precious duty to conserve these great institutions which occasioned in us the possibility of capturing our ideal.

There is, in other words, for us something dearer and holier even than our individual ideal: that is the possibility that *every* man should have the chance of finding an ideal and following it and being transformed by it. Only one thing is higher to me than our own ideal and that is *the* ideal, that great glorious spiritual realm in which all individuals, standing shoulder to shoulder, still look away from each other into diviner eyes, toward the Brotherhood of Idealists, toward the Communion of Saints, toward the Kingdom of God.

So far we may see that the great institutions are necessary. Thus does the loyalty to institutions become sanctified by the halo flung over them by the glory of our ideal. We revere them as well as we honor them. We support them because they foster, but only because they foster, the growth and spread of the ideal. They are, according to the Epistle of Peter, "lights shining in a dark place to which we do well to give heed, until the day dawns and the daystar arises in our hearts."

But when that star of the ideal rises, we can no longer be merely Churchmen or Statesmen or Schoolmen. We are then Sons of a living God, destined to the glory and agony and loneliness of free men. Like Christ, we revere and serve the State, the School, the Church and the Home, behind whose sturdy walls individual souls grow best into beauty and freedom. Yet we stand in the liberty wherewith every holy ideal makes a man free, and are not to be entangled in any yoke of bondage. God makes us all idealists who love the holy institutions of mankind. God gives us institutions which nourish and inspire the idealists of our or any time. Trust them, rather than fear them. There are no products nobler than they.

MORE THAN CONQUERORS

Who shall separate us from the love of Christ? Shall tribulation, or distress, or persecution, or famine, or nakedness, or peril, or sword? Nay, in all these things we are more than conquerors *through him that loved us.*

ROMANS 8:35, 37

XV "More Than Conquerors"

THAT is just like the Bible; it is always wanting something more. Isn't it hard enough to be conquerors? Why intimate that we ought to be something greater? That is one reason why we have shoved the Book so far back on our shelves. It is an extreme book; it asks the impossible. It might have had more influence over the years if it had been content with less. Shakespeare, for example, is so much wiser; even his noblest characters have consoling flaws in them. A man feels that he can perhaps make Shakespeare's grade.

But look at some of the Bible characters. One can live with Hamlet or King Lear or Othello a good deal more easily than with Peter, Paul or John. They fly too high; hence we turn away our eyes and take a train that runs on solid rails on solid ground, where other trains have run and where there are fewer wrecks. The Bible belongs with Plato's Dialogues in the world of unapproachable beauty. But it is worse than Plato, for Plato is mostly dreams and the Bible is mostly biography. Nobody ever lived like Plato's philosopher-kings. But Jesus and Paul and Stephen were men; they actually lived, and what they said or did or wrote is a challenging deposit of actual experience. They are most uncomfortable personages, living or dying, to have floating about the universe.

Sometimes, when Paul begins to boast a bit and to mention all the hurdles he has taken, we begin to think that he is like us after all, and we get ready to applaud him. But when he drops his voice and says, "Conquerors? Nay, more than conquerors," we're mystified—although we know we have ears, we know we hear not. What's the matter with Alexander the Great and Frederick the Great and the other Greats? Didn't they cut a big enough swath in the world, changing the entire course of history? Why should Paul, or anyone else, demand more?

Well, what about the Greek conqueror, Alexander of Macedon? It is hard to discover a better illustration of conqueror than he. He united East and West, it is true, but that is a mere side issue with him. What he lives for is just plain conquering, and always conquering in a fairly drawn-up battle so that everyone may know that a fight is going on. After his generals successfully bring up his great army to where a greater army of the enemy lies unprepared and sleeping and bid him charge and win, he spurns them and their strategy. Who would *steal* a victory? said he.

When at last he finds himself face to face with the main army of Darius and his valiant generals shudder with fear before the horde of Persians and scimitars and elephants, he lies down in peace and sleeps because he no longer has to *find* the enemy, but only to *fight* him. He loves the battle rather than the reward. When he addresses his chosen officers, he does not seek to beguile them with booty nor to ennoble them by the idea that they are carriers of Greek culture to barbarians. He spurs them on to conquest for the sheer joy of it. "The rewards of noble deeds," he cries, "are the deeds themselves."

Even the aid of his own soldiers is distasteful to him, for it robs him of the glory of single combat. He rebukes a friend of his for presuming to slay a lion that seemed to be about to kill him. He springs alone from the top of a walled city into the midst of his enemies, when the siege ladder breaks and the soldiers following him in the ascent are hurled back impotently. With amazement we watch his conspicuous white plume darting into the midst of peril and challenging every foe to bring on his best and taste the inevitable defeat. Unlike Frederick and Napoleon, he was never invaded by fear. When his father, Philip, was alive, he lamented his victories, for they meant so many less victories for himself. He is the only great general who never lost a battle. On every count he is conqueror *par excellence*. He is the very spirit of conquest incarnate, of daring that was never overmatched, of power that was never overborne.

Yet, as we recount such stirring deeds, is not the word that springs to our lips the word "dare-devil"? Does the supreme human conqueror really conquer us? Do not those of you who know Alexander best protest against this ill-balanced sketch of him that I have drawn? Do you not miss in the picture all those touches of magnanimity and affection and deep loyalty and strange monitions of the divine that make the allurement of Alexander? Will you not remind me that Alexander was something more than a conqueror, that he was a friend, an aspirer after God, an admirer of *all* human valor?

But then are you not suddenly confirming the language of the irritating Bible and joining with it in pointing us to something beyond the joy of standing alone, of measuring our might against our foes, and of conquering? Even the greatest conqueror in human history was more than that.

Or here is Frederick the Great, King of Prussia, rightly denounced yet always fascinating. What makes the fascination in him? Is it the leap over the Silesian boundary, with disciplined troops at his back, which changed the whole current of European life? Then he was on conquest bent. Cynically he pokes fun at his own claims of right. Frankly he confesses that the demon Fame has visited him and that he has welcomed her to his breast. And rather than lose the conquest that she inspired, he permitted Europe to be turned for seven years into a battlefield.

But it is surely not his agility in highway robbery, which he shared with many another monarch of his day, or his callousness in wholesale murder, or his brazen confession of unleashed ambition, that makes him a figure of enthralling interest to us. It is rather the ennoblement of his ambition by his love of country and by the pride of his country in him. It is the process by which his fame and that of Prussia became so completely interwoven that he could not separate one from the other. That is why, finally, he could write a secret letter to one of his ministers directing that, if he himself were captured, he should never be ransomed at the expense of his country, and that, if he were to be slain, the event should be disguised and the government proceed upon its even course as though merely a private had fallen.

"All men," said the king, "are created equal; the monarch is but a man whom the people have chosen to be their first servant." The fascination of Frederick and his meed of greatness lie in the fact that the great conqueror was at least partially conquered.

Does not, then, the contemplation of these conquerors lead us *beyond* their conquering? Do we not begin to sense the meaning of the text, that there *is* something higher than conquering? To conquer, to be sure, is much nobler than to drift; it indicates a will to rule, an energy that holds lesser powers in leash and releases them for a settled purpose. But there is something nobler still, and that is *being fitly conquered.* Is that not, indeed, part of the blessed secret with which Jesus startled the world? "Blessed are the poor in spirit, for theirs is the kingdom of heaven." Is it not at the heart of Paul's triumphant spirit? "When I am weak, then am I strong. Most gladly therefore will I glory in my infirmities, that the power of Christ may rest upon me."

A conqueror measures his strength by the inferiors whom he has defeated. A man is less than a conqueror who measures his strength by adversaries or passions which have downed him, and finds therefore his will overborne, his spirit captive, his purposes broken. A man is more than conqueror who finds himself invaded by a power not only stronger but dearer and nobler than his own, who finds himself not unclothed but clothed upon, his spirit changed but not broken, his purposes transformed and integrated into a worthier and more irresistible enterprise.

Do we not, my friends, draw our lines of demarcation between the great and the greatest by the distinction that the Apostle throws underneath this irritating text? Does not the spiritual gulf between the man who conquers jubilantly and the man who is divinely conquered explain the long life of the often misunderstood words "conversion" and "consecration"? Cant and hypocrisy have not been able to submerge those expressions by which men indicate the possibility of being changed from the state of self-confidence and self-possession into the state of being divinely possessed. Do we not covet, most of all, a belief in a power immeasurably transcending our own, and a sense of sharing it on its own terms?

This sense of successful escape from the limitations of self is what makes the record of a life like Curie's holy, though devoid of religion. In reading it, we realize how his powers were conquered by the secret forces of the universe. In order to live with them, he eschewed all converse with men of position lest he should be bound by life's amenities. His wife preserves the essence of the man in the sentence with which he was wont to end a meal or a rare conversation: "Come, let's get to work." With that she breaks off her short biography of her husband and goes off to *her* laboratory, thus evidencing her supreme devotion to the supreme object of his—conquered by the cosmic forces.

Some years ago I was moved by an account of this interior conquest in the political field. It was a reported conversation between a Mr. Barker and Sun Yat-sen, who was then President of China and who had not yet been entangled in the later messes of Chinese politics. Mr. Barker had said, "With a reward of $500,000 on your head you should not go alone through the deserted streets of a strange town." Sun Yat-sen, with a quiet smile, said in effect, "If they had killed me some years ago, it would have been a pity for the cause; then I was indispensable. Now my life does not matter. There are plenty of Chinese who are ready to take my place, now conquered by love of country."

Is it not so? Those whom we call good, those whom we most deeply envy, are those who have been clothed upon, so that what is their own has been swallowed up by that which belongs to us all, or rather by that to which we all belong.

May I quote a paragraph from Professor Harper's *Wordsworth*?

"It was the hour of his baptism with the fire of poesy, an hour memorable in his life and in the history of literature. It was the supreme religious moment of his life, the point when his being stood cut off for the first time from every human soul, the point, too, when by this very isolation his soul lay bare to divine influence and he communed with God, submissive to the heavenly voice. He then accepted—he could not help accepting—the call of a power beyond his control. And from that time his faculties were released. The incident does not admit of paraphrase and must be read in his own words, the momentous conclusion being:

'I made no vows, but vows
Were then made for me; bond unknown to me
Was given, that I should be, else sinning greatly,
A dedicated Spirit.' "

No wonder Wordsworth spells that word Spirit with a capital S. Conquered, you see, but conquered by a power he had longed to feel.

My mind reverts to antiquity and to the supreme Book. I behold the prophet Jeremiah sitting apart from men, debarred from the company of merry-makers, ostracized by the 100 per cent patriots, demanding that his weak and sinful people submit unconditionally to the mighty Babylonian conqueror, Nebuchadnezzar. Amid the jeers of men, and as from the slimy dungeon whence he was rescued only by the impulse of a slave, I hear him call to his God:

"Thou hast seduced me, O God,
And I was seduced.
I said to myself,
I will speak no more in his name.
But there burned, as it were, a fire in my bones,
And I could no longer contain.
O God, thou art stronger than I;
Over me thou hast prevailed."

I think of a predecessor of mine in my first pastorate. He presented himself in the city of Brooklyn for licensure. The members of the committee empowered to grant it began their examination on scattered and quivering points of theology. His answers and their questions alike seemed beside the mark to Henry Ward Beecher, who sat with them in counsel. Suddenly Dr. Beecher broke his silence and, bending over to my friend as though to sweep trivialities aside, he cried, "My brother, are you a slave to Love?" That question *was* an ordination.

Do you recall a line in the Book of Judges, which is not easily forgotten, "The Spirit of the Lord clothed itself with Gideon"? That is the sentence I wish might be written of you and of me. I wish that we might sublimate our natural desire for mastery in a consuming desire to be nobly mastered. To have that as the cardinal desire is in some sense to have it fulfilled. "Live seeking God," said Tolstoi, "and you will never live without him."

Let us pray. O Thou, whom no man hath seen or can see but who has come closest to us in Him who lived not to be ministered unto but to minister, wilt Thou not invade our souls and empower our faculties for their supreme task? Wilt Thou not dwell in our empty and longing hearts, giving us serenity and strength, and surrounding us, in the midst of our weakness and failures, with the peace and largeness of eternity?

Leave us not alone. Throw around our incompleteness Thy compassion and grace, beneath our restlessness Thy rest, beneath the abyss of death faith and hope and love.   Amen.

ON READING ONESELF

And behold a certain lawyer stood up and made trial of him, saying, Teacher, what shall I do to inherit eternal life? And Jesus said unto him, How readest thou?

LUKE 10:25–26

XVI On Reading Oneself
Into Eternal Life

WHAT an irritating and wholly irrelevant question Jesus here seems to make to a man who was asking one of the fundamental questions of human existence! The idea of asking a man, in personal trouble about his soul, what his reading habits were! But Jesus is not in the habit of asking silly questions, and so we are at once convinced that there is some vital connection between the things a man reads and his chances of eternal life. It is that connection which I wish to consider with you today. I wish to convince you, if I can, that the art of reading is not an idle ornament of life but a central and a determining portion of the career of the soul, changing its quality and influencing its destiny.

Obviously many of you are in quite different circumstances regarding reading from both the lawyer in our text and the present speaker. In the New Testament the lawyer is not a man who practised law at the Jewish bar, but one who was an expert in the Jewish *Torah*, contained principally in the first five books of the Bible. It was his profession, as it is mine, to read—his even more than mine. The first teaching of the text, then, is that a man's eternal life and a man's professional life are closely connected.

If one of you business men should now ask Jesus what you are to do to inherit eternal life, he would ask you, if he treated you as he did this young man, "How do you conduct your business? What are your plans for increasing it? Do they rest fundamentally on wiser and better commercial methods, or on some subtle way of outwitting competitors, with no appreciable gain for anybody except yourself? What have you done, in other words, to connect your portion of human life with its eternal values?"

Or if one of you mothers should ask him how you might enter into eternal life, he might ask you, "What is it that charms you most in your children? What side of their little souls are you trying to bring out?" Or, if a teacher should ask the same question, Jesus might respond, "Well, how are you treating your pupils? Are you looking upon them as so many necessary but regrettable incidents in making your living, or as so many chances to connect your life and their lives with the vast and amazing secrets of the universe which you have inherited together?" Evidently in Jesus' mind eternal life and professional life are closely interrelated.

But I wish to pass over that somewhat familiar teaching of our text in favor of the connection that exists between *reading* and inheriting life. For in many a passage Jesus makes it clear that it was not only the lawyers whom he assumed to be vitally interesting in reading the religious classics of their age.

To begin with, then, however our actions may foolishly belie our opinions, I presume that there is nobody in this House of Worship today who would not be prepared to admit that the main business of living is to make some personal and assured connection with the eternal life, the sense of the divine within human life. We completely fail in living if we miss that sense. The man who lives the largest and most exalted life is the one who lives most in touch with God. Significantly, it is worth noting that the relation of a man to this eternal life is expressed in the text as the verb *inherit*. We do not *earn* eternal life. We do not ourselves create it. We enter it—we inherit it.

Jesus once remarked, "Unless we receive the Kingdom of God as little children, we can in no wise enter therein." Children get the best they have, indeed almost all they have, not by earning it nor by making it but by taking it. It is there, and they make connections with it. They inherit life, they inherit love, they inherit a home and talents and brains and truth. "What is there that thou hast," says Paul, "that thou hast not received?" If love and faith and mystery and right and truth are inherent parts of human life, we inherit them just as much as we inherit the sky and the stars and the night and the strange gift of sleep. The indispensable underlying realities of human life come to us as children, not as fighters. We are not to storm eternal life; we are to ask for it, to seek it, to take it. Eternal life is an inheritance.

But *how* do we inherit it? There are two answers to this question, and have been for centuries. They have shaped much of the philosophical and theological history of the race. One answer is, We inherit eternal life as a fresh, unmeditated gift from God. The other answer is, We inherit it from God but through the long line of our spiritual forbears. I presume that most of us in this age, which believes so strongly in development, would take the latter view. The birth of Jesus may have been an exception, but to most of us it has made a vast difference not only what sort of God we had but what sort of mother and father we had. But we are no more dependent upon our parents than our parents were on theirs, and so we begin to understand why it is that we are said to *inherit* eternal life. The divine life did not begin, even for us, with our birth. We came into the divine life through a vast miracle, but it was here before we were.

But, my friends, inheriting the eternal life is not simply a matter of being born. It depends rather upon the extent of our own spiritual capital, our visions, our aspirations, our repentances, our humility, our prayers. And these things depend chiefly upon the greatness of the souls with whom we have contact, and the largeness of the truth in whose presence we are living. The extent of our possessions in the realm of the eternal life hinges upon our acquaintance with Truth and inspiring Personality. And this depends largely upon the books we read and how we read them.

There is nothing more fatal to a man's outlook upon life than to acquiesce in the superficial contrast that is often drawn between life and books. There are, of course, books that put you to sleep, but there are also addresses and sermons that put you to sleep, and there are even persons who put you to sleep—or worse. Books and life are alike in that they both contain very dull spots. But they are alike at a more vital point—they are both products of the spirit.

You will come into contact with far more dynamic life in the Book of Amos than in the crowded stadium of a football game. People about us speak and think all the time, but those who are most in earnest in their thinking write their thoughts down in orderly and consecutive fashion. People about us wonder about the world in which they live, but those who wonder to some purpose, and attempt to test their wonder by its conformity to the outer universe, are those who write down their adventures with truth. People about us are all the time in the midst of the most marvelous experiences; they feel themselves face to face with unexpected crises of the spirit, stirred by duty and need, glorified by love, threatened by confusion, shamed by sin. But those who out of such experiences find new roads for the soul to travel, new and self-authenticating visions of God, new and transforming power for human need, are the pioneers of the spirit who write down their experiences in morality and recount their communion with God.

And after the thinkers and the scientists and the prophets have written down their true accounts of their unusual discoveries, the great and unerring judge, Time, sifts all these many documents of life and separates them into two very disparate groups. There is a large one with the multitudinous souls whose experiences, interesting as they may be, are yet dispensable; and there is a small one containing the exceedingly few first-hand, essential, original personalities and discoveries whereby we live.

The longer Time has to work, the more unimpeachable are his judgments. That is the reason why Emerson said he never read a book that was not at least ten years old. He knew there would be a good many he need never read if he waited for even ten years to test their worth. A book that is a century old and that still lives, you may be sure, is worth while. And a book that is two thousand years old and lives as no other book has ever lived, you may well put in a place by itself and determine that if you read no other book you will read at least that, not because it is the oldest, not because of its antiquarian or historic interest, but because Time has shown that it is more alive, more indispensable, more dynamic, more modern than all the yellowing manuscripts that have appeared and disappeared since. The longer a book has lived, the more it is likely to lead you into the secrets of eternal life.

The three greatest books I have ever read are all of them two thousand years old—the Bible, the memorabilia of Socrates as preserved by Plato, and the annals of Confucius. They live and they make me live because they introduce me to the most revolutionizing personalities of human history, men who have remade the centuries and who remake my soul. We should have said that these last two thousand years should have produced spirits of equal power and authority and beauty, but the "Spirit bloweth where it listeth," and if we are after the Spirit, we must be where it blows. I do not mean to say that there are not many men who have not uttered thoughts, recorded divine guesses at the riddle of existence as worthy as many words of Paul or Socrates, but their thoughts and guesses do not betray that rare mark of original power as do those five or six personalities that Time has separated from all others, as the deepest wells that spring up into eternal life.

If you desire the water of life, you must draw it from its own springs or take the trouble to connect your life with its great reservoirs by adequate pipes. And you must make time for it. It is worth sacrificing a business investment, hours of open air, skill at chess or cards, to obtain. At any rate, you have no right to complain of the shallowness of life if you refuse to make so obviously rewarding a sacrifice.

It is absolutely impossible for you to understand and to appreciate, as you well might, the vast horizons and the unplumbed depths and the mysterious shimmering beauty of human life unless you have stood by the side of Confucius and Buddha, or of Amos and Hosea and Job and Paul, unless you have knelt in the presence of Jesus Christ. If you refuse the ridiculously small sacrifices necessary to this end, you sin against your own soul, against the children of your home whose atmosphere your soul creates, and against all that large circle of the community which you help to influence.

Before I close, I wish to prove to you that reading yourself into a far larger inheritance into eternal life is by no means impossible for the busiest clerk, the most burdened business-man, the most wearied and occupied mother, except of course at those unusual hours of stress when illness or crisis or weakness forbid even a half hour's leisure to the spirit.

It is interesting to note that we are a reading people in a far greater degree than any people who have preceded us. And to a considerable degree we read valuable matter. Who is there of us who does not read the daily paper? And I hope there are few of us who belittle it. It takes us out of our own narrow and egotistic problems; it brothers us with all mankind; it broadens our horizons; it enlarges and enriches our personalities; it makes us all share in the universal life of our times and puts us in possession of the joy and sorrows, of the aspirations and struggles and obstacles of mankind.

If our paper is not unduly partisan, it brings us into touch with the most outstanding and inspiring personalities of our time. That is what we must demand of our paper, a chance to look at the great contemporary figures, not to look at the caricature but the actual countenance of the men who are leading the various sections of our people and of other peoples. And, as we obtain that chance, our own interests will grow more and more into the human interests, and we will learn to trust and to rejoice in many a direction where we cannot follow.

And these papers and one or two good magazines enable us to hold our place in our worlds, the world of affairs with its moral values; the world of science with its continual reminder of the greatness and the vast orderliness and surpassing mystery of the universe in which we are so miraculously dropped and so marvelously at home; the world of philosophic thought, revealing to us so clearly the limitations of reason but also the sure grounds and the imperative necessity of faith. It is the daily and weekly and monthly papers and periodicals—one of each of which should be in every home—which make the lives of the busiest of us so interesting, so satisfactory, so broad, so human.

And with what a small expenditure of time we gain this large participation in the great currents of human life! A few minutes in the car or at the table, and the scope of our life has been enlarged and we have entered into that eternal current of human destiny which is our divine inheritance. It is not necessary to read for hours; it is only necessary to read with attention and with humility and with a teachable and expectant spirit. Even here the question is not, "How long readest thou?" Much more important is the question Jesus put to the young man, "*How* readest thou?"

Let us remember, however, that Jesus' question was not, "What is written in the daily paper?" It was not even what was written in the latest apocalypse or collection of the wisdom literature that was stirring his contemporaries. It was, "What is written *in the law*, how readest thou?" You say you want eternal, divine life; how have you used that Book in which you believe the divine life has come to its most sacred and fullest impression? How have you made connection between your own life and the highest life you know? For some of us, the question would inevitably read, "What is written in the Gospel, how readest thou?" If we are to read ourselves into eternal life, we shall get furthest by an intimate and grateful use of the Gospels of our Lord and Saviour.

But do not mistake the question! It is not "how long" but "*how*" readest thou. Reading oneself into life eternal so that one breathes its atmosphere and feels its currents and rejoices in its God is not a thing that depends upon minutes and hours, but upon purpose and expectation. It does require ten of life's best minutes in the morning, when the brain is fresh, or twenty at night when the heart is serene; but, when one thinks of the reward, one knows that the main thing cannot be the expenditure of a short period of time but the investment of genuine longing and deepest hope.

As I have often said to young people, one of Boston's leading men told me once that what determined his life was his resolution when in college to keep himself in sight of the highest by reading a paragraph from the Gospels every day. A man who is reading for life will, it goes without saying, not read conventionally, allowing himself to be bound by definite verses or to think that their mere reading is an act of piety that has its own reward. But neither will he read too critically. It is a great service that competent Bible scholars have shown that not all parts of the Bible, nor even of the Gospels, are of equal value, and that there are errors or inadequacies in the Bible as in other books. But there is no use in dwelling on what the Bible has in common with other books; we should rather emphasize that which distinguishes it from virtually all others.

Therefore, we read the Bible not for the sake of pointing out its errors but for the sake of finding its life. At the beginning of each day, let us read that sacred book until we come into a realization of the sanctity of human life, the love and reality of God, and feel within ourselves that gratitude and good-will which prepare us for the tasks God has set down for us. There is no other book so enlarging, so illuminating, so full of preparation for modern tasks. It informs as much as the daily paper; it transforms a hundred-fold more.

Friends, let this one fact be perfectly clear to you: it is hypocrisy to believe that you are in earnest about the eternal life of the spirit if you neglect to acquaint yourselves with those words and those spirits in which the eternal life has built its tabernacles. The man who asks the first question of the text, "What shall I do to inherit eternal life?" should hear clearly the second question as we have modified it, "What is written in the Gospels, how readest thou?"

Would that I could be assured that no member of this congregation can feel satisfied without bringing his life every morning to the judgment seat of the Gospels, to the refreshment and power of the Gospels! And would that we all, when we read them and the great messages of

the prophets and the tender prayers of the Psalms and the matchless letters of St. Paul, may not think of ourselves as searching an ancient book,
but as coming into the company of those across the centuries, in whose
faces we are still able to catch the light of the knowledge of the glory of
God.

SOSTHENES OUR BROTHER

Paul, called to be an apostle of Jesus Christ through the will of God, and Sosthenes our brother . . .

I CORINTHIANS I:I

XVII "Sosthenes Our Brother"

O F these two men, Paul is by far the more important. It is quite proper that his insights, his courage, his faith, his efficiency, should be made the theme of numberless sermons and books. But it took both Paul and Sosthenes to produce the first letter to the Corinthians. It is one of the great treasures of Christendom, perhaps the greatest example of epistolary literature in the world; and this morning I wish to direct your attention to Sosthenes and his share in enriching our Christian heritage. Many people have thought that he was the same Sosthenes, the ruler of the synagogue in Corinth, who was beaten by a frenzied mob before the judgment seat of Gallio (Acts 18:17). But we shall not attempt to delve into his past; I wish simply to call your attention to the unique importance of Sosthenes as this letter reveals it.

Paul and Sosthenes! How much better a letter they turned out than Paul and Peter could possibly have done! Wilson and Marshall, for example, provided a much more efficient administration in Washington than Woodrow Wilson and Theodore Roosevelt could possibly have given us. It is no accident that the vice-president has become an essentially colorless individual. You cannot get as good results in great undertakings if you have two men of genius yoked together as if you have one man of genius and another man who adores him. If any of you happen to be a vice-president of anything, remember that your function is to carry out the policy of the president when you approve of it and to remain silent if you don't.

Just suppose Paul and Peter had sat down together to write this letter to the Church in Corinth! It would not have been long before Peter would have asked Paul if he meant just what he said; if he didn't think that this was rather hard to be understood, somewhat over the heads of the church, perhaps not quite in the spirit of Christ, or not properly respectful to the law. Why, the letter would have been full of compromises and rich in platitudes. For if you get two men of independent genius to write something together, both accustomed to leadership and both fully convinced in their own minds and even though full of the spirit of Christian love, you are sure to have a flat, profitless document, against which nothing can be said and about which, after the first reading, nothing ever will be said.

Paul and Sosthenes made a very much better evangelistic team than Paul and Peter, or Paul and Apollos, could have made. Do not be disgruntled if you are only a Sosthenes. If you can find a Paul, you will actually be of more use to him than if you were a Peter. Sosthenes did not try to tell Paul what to write; he left that to the Holy Spirit. The first thing for every Sosthenes to learn is that he isn't Paul; nay, if he has to learn it, he will not be a Sosthenes. It is only to a Sosthenes, not to a Peter, that Paul can say what Shakespeare's Ulysses said to Nestor: "I have a young conception in my brain. Be you my time to bring it to some shape."

Sosthenes wrote a letter which is still the wonder and inspiration of the world, because he let Paul write it. The first thing for every amanuensis to learn is that his task is to write down what is said to him, not to improve it. In fact, that is the first requisite of all good workmen, never to mistake themselves for their employers. The place of all workingmen is to carry out some one else's policy, not to tinker it, to criticize it, or to improve it. The only thing for an employer to do with a workman who is always doing something better than he's told is to discharge him. There can be only one head of a responsible and effective business. The letter to the Corinthians was a success because Paul did the thinking and Sosthenes the writing.

And, my friends, permit me to say here that this is the reason why so many of us get along badly as Christian disciples: we tinker Christ's program instead of following it out. And that is the reason why it is so important for us to think of Sosthenes. We may be the Paul in some line—in business, in politics, or in art; but in the fundamental relationship of life we are all Sosthenes. One is our Master, even Christ; and each one of us is a Sosthenes, a brother.

But Sosthenes did more than write this letter to the Corinthian Church; he saved Paul's strength to write other letters. If Paul had strained his wretched eyes, and cramped his ungainly hands and exhausted his invaluable time by writing in his big characters, he would have written a poorer letter; he would have had less energy to release in his next speech; he would have been depressed at falling below his own standard, and eventually he would have dried up. When the Sosthenes are exhausted, the Pauls will be.

The civil and electrical engineers can do nothing without the boatloads of immigrant laborers that some of them are inane enough to cudgel and despise. The architect in his neatly appointed office, and with his head bent over his blueprints, is absolutely dependent, for his chance to live and work upon men, upon those who can be depended upon to carry his plans into effect. The vast railroad and aviation enterprises, the telephone and the telegraph systems are planned on the assumption that there will always be men willing and able to run them. Upon the supply of our Sosthenes the stability of the world depends; upon an occasional Paul, its progress. We must have both, and we must have cooperation between both. It is the presence and the fidelity of the Sosthenes in the world which make possible the presence and the glory of the Pauls.

Is it any wonder, then, that the first words which Sosthenes the amanuensis was bidden, by Paul the genius, to write were these: "Paul . . . an apostle of Jesus Christ . . . , and Sosthenes our brother." I am sure that Sosthenes was not surprised to hear the first words of that phrase; but he might have been surprised indeed at the last words. I think they were both rare Christians and firm friends, but I am sure his face flushed with pleasure as he heard Paul say, "Sosthenes our brother." And as he wrote it down, it was not the word "Sosthenes" that rejoiced his heart, but the word "brother." After that word had been said, as Paul would have said it, he was no longer a servant, an employee, but a partner in a task of great moment. His work was not Paul's, but Paul's work depended upon his and Paul knew it.

There can be no doubt about it: only the recognition of the brotherhood on the part of both Paul and Sosthenes can bring peace between the employers and the employees of the world and efficiency in their undertakings. But such an announcement would bring more than peace; it would bring joy—joy of which now our nerves are scant. If we can find employers who will say "Sosthenes our brother" in the tone that Paul said it, we will have a crowd of Sosthenes who rejoice that they can save, and that they alone can save, our Pauls. Sosthenes knew that he was saving Paul's strength not for Paul's sake, but for the Gospel's sake. The secret of success in any business is to have a body of workmen who are sure that the product of their toil is not merely to fill the employer's pocket, but to develop efficiency in the great enterprise upon which they are engaging together.

But Sosthenes' service to Paul went even further than this. He not only saved his strength for other letters, but he enriched Paul for the writing of this one. Sosthenes was not only an amanuensis or, as we would say, a stenographer, but he was a Christian. He was Paul's brother not only because he shared Paul's faith. He felt somewhat of the splendor of the letter Paul was writing. But as Paul looked at his stenographer, impatiently perhaps to see if he had caught up to him, or hesitating over a sentence, or wondering if what he had said was plain, he found before him an unconscious judge. Paul didn't have to imagine his audience; he had one. And he could tell by Sosthenes' face whether he had done his task well or ill, whether the Corinthians would be able to understand or not.

It was just as well, probably for them and for us, that Sosthenes was there. It held Paul down to the earth. He couldn't go faster than Sosthenes could write, and unconsciously he would find himself increasingly unwilling to go faster than Sosthenes could understand. I have little doubt that some of the intricacies of Paul's style, his peculiar use of prepositions, and his manner of leaving a sentence before it was finished to go on with the next, were due to the simple fact that Sosthenes did not get all of it down. By some ejaculation or the sound of a despairing dig into the papyrus this became known to Paul, and he went more slowly and thoughtfully. When Sosthenes did not get the sense, the bewilderment came out in his face, and Paul was doubtless forced to make another and a more successful try. A considerable bit of self-discipline and suppressed irritation underlay the ecstatic course of Paul's thought, gave it substance and coherence.

There can be no doubt, moreover, when Sosthenes did understand and saw that the intricacies of the moral and ecclesiastical situation had been cleared up, that his face lit up, and that there was a warmth in the little room which urged Paul on to greater insights and more enduring flights. I have no doubt that Sosthenes was a channel for much of the inspiration of the Holy Spirit that is so evident in the epistle. We shall never know how much the presence of the stenographer had to do with such a passage as, "Behold your calling, brethren, that not many wise, not many mighty, not many noble, are called"; or such a passage as, "The eye cannot say to the hand, I have no need of thee"; or how much the fervor and joy of his spirit helped Paul to write "Love is kind, it envieth not; it vaunteth not itself, is not puffed up, doth not behave itself unseemly." But Sosthenes *had* his part. If Paul had been alone in the room, the letter would certainly not have had the weight, the glow, the depth which the presence of Sosthenes imparted to it.

How ministers, authors, artists, teachers understand what the Sosthenes do for them! As they work, they say to themselves: so-and-so will be appreciative but this is not clear enough for him; of this another will not approve; to a third that will have to be re-written, for it is not worthy of his eye. And this is true in all lines of business. I am confident that many a store-keeper lays in a certain kind of stock because he unwittingly is influenced by the taste of his discriminating clerks: that many a shady transaction is abandoned because the proprietor is ashamed to have his tradespeople take part in it; that many a teacher restrains her temper, or puts another half-hour upon her work, because she wants to live up to the standard which she knows some Sosthenes in her room takes for granted; that many a mother will confess that her child has brought her up fully as much as she has brought up her child.

Ah, valuable as the Pauls are in the world, it is the Sosthenes who enrich them, keep them up. Every once in a while a man will say, "Oh, what a relief it will be when she (one of my clerks) gets back." Once my best pupil employed the hour, when I was lecturing on Napoleon, in writing an overdue theme; the whole hour was shorn of its delight, for I had fallen down in my capacity as Paul. What a difference it makes to the entire household if the right maid is in the kitchen, or, to the anxious watchers, if the proper nurse is at the bedside. It only requires the right servant in the house, the right tenant on the third floor back, the right student in the class, the right stenographer in the office, to have the atmosphere change. I hope the Sosthenes know it, and I hope the Paul's say "our brother" in a way that makes them know it.

We probably spend little time in trying to decide whether we belong with Paul or Sosthenes. A Paul comes once in a thousand years; Sosthenes are born every day. There may be, indeed, one or two among us who remind the rest of us of Paul, but even they are Pauls in only one function; for in most of their time they are Sosthenes. Nobody leads as much as he leans. In all departments of life, save perhaps one in which we may have some authority, we depend upon others; at one point we may be like Paul, and at all others like Sosthenes. That is to say, human life is fundamentally a Sosthenes' affair. The awareness of dependence is far more necessary and determinative with us than any attitude of command.

It was so even with Paul. His greatest joy was not in pronouncing weighty decisions as an authoritative apostle to the Corinthians, but in the feeling that his Master was speaking through him as he spoke through Sosthenes. The joy of apostleship was indeed great, but the joy of being a bondslave of Christ was far greater: "It is no more I that live but Christ that liveth in me; the love of Christ constraineth me; the life I live in the flesh I live by faith in Christ who loved me and gave himself for me."

If any of us is failing in joy or in a worthy feeling of satisfaction in life, it is not because we fail of being a Paul; it is because we fail of being a Sosthenes. That which empties life of significance is not that we cannot lead but that we are not conscious of being led worthily. What makes our life seem futile is not that we have no one under us, but that we have no one over us. We can easily renounce the thought of using others for our aims, but life loses its glory when we are no longer conscious of being used for a purpose far beyond our power. Sosthenes all, we come to our majestic own, only when we find ourselves saying with our fathers:

> Lord, thou hast been our dwelling place in all generations;
> Before the mountains were brought forth
> Or ever thou hadst formed the earth and the world,
> Even from everlasting to everlasting thou art God.
> Let the beauty of the Lord our God be upon us,
> And establish thou the work of our hands upon us.
> Yea, the work of our hands, establish thou it.

500 copies printed in November, 1955, at
The Stinehour Press · Lunenburg, Vermont